HOW TO
NEGOTIATE
BETTER DEALS

HOW TO
NEGOTIATE
BETTER DEALS

Jeremy G. Thorn

Copyright © 1989, 1991 Jeremy G. Thorn

First published in 1989 by Mercury Books
Reprinted in paperback 1991

Reprinted May 1994 by Management Books 2000 Ltd
125A The Broadway, Didcot, Oxfordshire OX11 8AW

Text cartoons by Keith Reynolds

Set in Concorde by Phoenix Photosetting, Chatham, Kent
Printed and bound in Great Britain by BPC Wheatons Ltd, Exeter

British Library Cataloguing in Publication Data is available

ISBN 1-85252-069-8

PREFACE

'There was a time when a fool and his money were soon parted,
but now it happens to everybody.' *Adlai Stevenson*

How to Negotiate Better Deals will help all those who have to
negotiate as part of their job, whether they are buying, selling or
manufacturing, in administration or in general management.
More broadly, readers will find that these negotiating skills can
be employed not just at work, but at home and on holiday, with
the family and neighbours, shopkeepers and bank managers, the
tax man, Town Hall, and wherever else opportunities exist to
negotiate a better deal.

The practical advice and help that is offered is based on years
of negotiating experience from around the world. This book tells
you not only *how* to negotiate, but *why*, *when* and *where*. It
covers the strategies of both cooperative and competitive
bargaining, as well as how to handle confrontation. There is
detailed discussion on how to ensure that you win the best deal
in each case, how to promote mutual gain and how to avoid a
shared loss. A vast array of tactics is discussed, which might be
used by you – or against you!

Since its first publication, interest has been shown in this book
from countries in every continent, where indeed much of the
original source material came from in the first place. Negotiating
skills, and the interest in acquiring them, clearly know no
boundaries.

Equally gratifying has been the interest shown not just from industry and the broader business community, which includes bankers, insurance companies and lawyers, but also workers in local government, teachers and educationalists, doctors, social workers, those in leisure management, journalists and indeed almost all walks of life.

I hope you will feel this book will enable you, too, to negotiate better deals.

JEREMY G. THORN
Sheffield, England
April 1991

ACKNOWLEDGEMENTS

My grateful thanks go to all those who have assisted in producing this book, especially to those, whether wittingly or otherwise, who have provided the stimulus for some of the ideas. These include, among many others:

Mike Acaster, Fernando Alaña, Vic Archer, George Armitage, Bill Bacon, Trevor Baugh, Uli Brackelmann, Stuart Brayne, Andy Cawley, John Chesney, Monica Chrusander, Sue Cooke, Ray Durman, Eberhard Eickenbusch, Rachel Eli, Paul Ellis, Mike Evans, David Eyre, Brian Farrington, Tony Fazackerley, Jessica Frances, Fred Freund, Terry Gillatt, Stephanie Grace, Dick Higgs, Alan Hodson, Ian Hosea, Des Kavanagh, Ali Khalili, Jeremy Kinghorn, Barry Knott, Alison Lakin, Bertrand Lapostolle, Chris Leake, Armand Lehmann, Alicen Marie, Enrico Mariotti, Walter Nimmo, Juan Nuñes, Nils Olin, Chandra Patel, Philippe Pétitfrère, Henry Plant, Robert Postema, Chris Boydell, Maggie Rowlands, Hugh Sharp, Peter Shipway, Eric Sjørman, Patricio de la Sota, Connard Stitzlein; Daphne, Éilis, Pat and Robin Thorn; Philip Walker, Peter Warr, Nigel Watkins.

Special thanks must also go to Roger Thorn, LL.B.(Hons), Barrister-at-Law of the North Eastern Circuit, not only for his twin-brotherly inspiration and support, but more particularly for his legal contributions. Commentary on UK law is stated as applicable up to late 1988.

Finally, I offer my warmest appreciation to Keith Reynolds for so successfully bringing the cartoon captions to life (including those which were *not* used on the grounds of good taste and public sensitivity).

CONTENTS

WHY NEGOTIATE?

'Let us never negotiate out of fear. But let us never fear to
negotiate.'

Inaugural address – President John F. Kennedy.

This book is about how to negotiate better deals: not just about
the mechanics of how negotiation works, but about the ways it
can work for *you*. How do you become more successful at it?
How can you avoid failure or disappointment? How, indeed, can
we all do better when we have to do a deal?

Now this assumes that everyone will naturally want to do
better. *You* probably do, in which case you will already have
some idea of what negotiation is and why people use it. You will
also know that when negotiations are conducted professionally,
significant improvements in the results are possible. You may
sometimes feel an understandable nervousness about entering a
negotiation, but that is only because of your uncertainty about
whether you can match the other side's skills. That is why you
bought this book. For you, a negotiation is an interesting challenge rather than, as some would say, an assault on good manners and personal integrity.

If all this applies to you, you don't need to be persuaded further
that negotiating is worthwhile; please feel free to go directly to
the summary at the end of this chapter. You already know the
benefits of doing better. What you want to know is how you can
achieve them.

WHY NEGOTIATE?

Not everyone, however, will possess this same confidence in the value of negotiating. You might be wondering if you really do want to learn how to negotiate more successfully. Why bother to negotiate at all?

To answer this, put yourself in the position of having to do a deal with somebody. You might want to buy, or to sell. You might want someone to do some work for you, or you might be asked to do some work for someone else. You *could* simply ask for an offer and accept it in good faith, but there is a problem here. Good faith can be abused. How do you *know* that the offer is fair or reasonable? More importantly, how do you know that the offer is *the best you could possibly get?* The answer to both questions is that more often than not, you don't.

The only way you can find out is by trying to win a better deal. On some occasions, this will indeed be second nature to you. You wouldn't accept the first offer you were to receive for the trade-in value of your car, would you? When you find your dream house, would you expect to buy without questioning the initial asking price? As with cars or houses, so with many other deals, and this leads neatly to the first basic fact about negotiating:

The first offer you get will rarely be the best possible. The only way to establish what *might* be the best deal is to negotiate.

But perhaps you still feel uncomfortable. Is it possible that you have a sneaking suspicion that negotiation is based on dis-honesty? Do you suspect that when *other* people negotiate, they are trying to win something which is almost certainly undeserved or unfair? And that if they succeed it is most probably through the use of some underhand negotiating tricks? (Indeed, tricks that you might suspect were learned from a book such as this!) Do you feel that when *you* end up in a negotiation, you have been forced to bargain in order to make others give you what was rightfully yours in the first place? Many do.

If you feel this way, perhaps it isn't really very surprising. Stories which enter popular folklore constantly reinforce the point of view that negotiation is largely about trickery. For example, do you know this story that was popular some years ago?

Some years after the Russian Revolution, a senior member of the Russian Praesidium was invited to visit Henry Ford's factory while on a tour of the USA. Wishing to make a grand gesture from the American people, Ford offered to give his distinguished Russian visitor the very next car to roll off his production line. The Russian declined. This would be an insult to the Russian people, he said, but he would certainly consider purchasing one. Immediately, Mr Ford generously offered to sell him the car for 50 cents. 'Wonderful!' replied the Russian with a beaming smile. He took a dollar bill out of his wallet and said: 'I'll take two.'

It is almost as if the Eastern Bloc countries have the best stories of this genre. Here is another one:

There were once two East German border-guards, who spent their time patrolling the boundary between their motherland and the decadent West. One day, looking longingly over the frontier towards all sorts of imagined delights, one sentry said to the other: 'Would you shoot me if I ran across to the other side?'
'Well, I would have to', replied the second sentry. 'It would be my duty.'
'OK,' said the first sentry, 'You go first.'

If stories such as these have given you the feeling that negotiation is about being sly, or even dishonest, please be reassured. Contrary to your expectations, perhaps, mutual trust between the parties involved is a basic requirement for a successful negotiation. The skills of negotiation are rarely 'tricks', nor generally underhand, and these skills are available to everyone. Negotiating skills can be readily taught, and the effort to learn and develop them will seem more worthwhile to those who know the second basic fact about negotiating:

Negotiators with the greatest skills will regularly conclude better deals than those who are less accomplished.

3

A basic requirement for success is trust.

Even though you may accept the above comments in good faith, you may still not be convinced that acquiring the skills of negotiating is worth your time and effort. You may feel that this is all a rather specialised activity which is not part of 'normal' people's lives. World powers may negotiate peace treaties with

4

each other and trade union leaders may bargain for better wage deals with 'the bosses', but surely, you might think to yourself, most of us are never going to need special skills on how to negotiate? That's for the experts, isn't it?

Perhaps negotiation *should* be left to experts. Good deals are so easily spoilt by poor negotiation skills. But these skills are readily accessible, and they can be used far more often than most people realise. We could all be experts if we wished. Therefore an important objective of this book will be to demonstrate another basic fact about negotiating:

Opportunities for negotiating better deals are all around us, all the time.

We may never have to bargain for the release of a terrorist's hostage or negotiate a superpower arms deal. But on a lesser scale we all *have* to negotiate on occasions. Frequently, for most of us, there are routine matters that need to be negotiated in our domestic lives. (Some of these will be mentioned in the next chapter, 'When to Negotiate'.) For many of us, negotiation will also be a functional requirement of the job we do, whether we are involved with buying and selling, for example, or managing those who work with and for us (as well as those we work *for*!).

Consider also the following examples of domestic deal-making which might be heard any day up and down the country. They all indicate negotiating situations:

'You can have some ice-cream if you eat up your vegetables.'
'You can play with my new football if I can borrow your pen.'
'I'll show you mine if you show me yours.'
'I'll tell my Dad if you hit me again.'
'If you work hard and pass your exams, we'll buy you a new bike.'
'You can go out tonight if you promise to be back by eleven.'
'I'll tell you, if you won't tell anyone else.'
'Will you wash the car if I mow the lawn?'
'I don't mind going to a beach for our holidays if we can spend at least one day walking in the hills.'
'If you don't mind working late tonight, you can come to work later tomorrow morning.'
'Why do you always give me the dirty jobs to do?'

5

'Is there any price reduction for payment in cash?'
'I can't pay you this week. Will next weekend do?'
'If you can't give me a rise now, what about a performance-related bonus scheme?'
'I shan't pay you until you've mended it properly.'
'What discount will you give me if I buy two?'

While the style and environment of these different proposals clearly varies enormously – about which I will say more in due course – the basic skills of successful negotiators are invariably the same. These skills are not 'trade secrets', nor are they devious.

Nevertheless, some people always seem to be more able negotiators than others, whether they are just 'street-wise' or have spent time formally studying and practising these skills.

It would clearly be useful to us all if we knew better just what skills a strong negotiator should have, and how they can most advantageously be applied.

This is exactly what this book will tell you, in the following chapters. First, however, some clarification is in order.

WHAT IS NEGOTIATION?

Negotiation is a much-abused word. It is *not* another term for selling. Both the relevant skills and the appropriate circumstances are quite different for these two activities. Negotiation may, on specific occasions, follow as a *consequence* of selling, but even then it will be a quite separate activity. Indeed, a complaint made by many sales people is that whilst they are taught to sell, they are rarely given the back-up skills to negotiate. For example, a buyer may wish to deal, but not under the conditions which the sales person may wish (or be allowed) to offer. At this stage, selling skills may be irrelevant. What is required here, to conclude a successful deal, is bargaining skills.

To fully understand the difference, note that selling is primarily about satisfying a specific customer's perceived needs, usually on a competitive basis against other suppliers, in exchange for money, but *negotiation is concerned with resolving conflict between two or more parties, usually by the exchange of con-cessions.* It can be competitive, known as *win-lose* negotiation, or it can be cooperative, known as *win-win.* We shall look at the differences between *win-win* and *win-lose* negotiations later.

On a philosophical level, it could be argued that a free society cannot function without negotiation: it provides an escape route, immensely preferable to fisticuffs or warfare, for the resolution of disputes and conflicts. On this basis, it is the social duty of all citizens to be as good negotiators as possible, as well as a form of enlightened self-interest.

Naturally, the task of all negotiators should be to maximise their own side's benefits, but this can only be done if an agreement can ultimately be reached. Like selling, negotiation requires the good will of both sides. If unreasonable demands are made by one side, the other does not have to accede. If necessary, the offended party can always choose to break off discussions altogether.

Accordingly, if there is going to be a negotiation, both sides should be able to obtain some benefit. As a consequence, short of anti-social behaviour and downright dishonesty (which is possible in any activity between two or more people), neither side should have to end up fundamentally worse off than before they started, other than through their own misjudgement or incompetence.

This view may emphasise theory, rather than the practice which we shall also look at in due course, but the important point is that **negotiation should be regarded as a potentially beneficial activity for both parties.** It is not only the lubricant of trade, but also of many other social interactions.

CULTURAL INHIBITIONS AND MISCONCEPTIONS

Given the guidelines set out above, most people will find that they do indeed wish to improve their negotiating power. Given this motivation, it would then be most convenient if we could all expect to conclude breathtakingly better deals simply by acquiring the core skills and then, perhaps, polishing them with some practice.

Unfortunately, this is unlikely to be possible. Before these new skills can be applied successfully, and even before they can be learned, we have to recognise some fundamental inhibitions and misconceptions which many acquire from early childhood. These can easily keep any potential negotiator from truly *wanting* to win a better deal.

What happens is that when the opportunities for negotiating present themselves, many of us simply lose courage. This may be due to any of several reasons, which are probably quite closely linked:

The fear of personal rejection. We don't like to ask for something and take the risk of being turned down, thus losing 'face' or goodwill. The consequence is that, rather than say 'No, that is not acceptable,' we prefer to concede or turn a blind eye. Only by recognising that brinkmanship can be a useful feature of negotiating is it possible to overcome this fundamental block to wanting to win a better deal.

The fear of being disliked. In general, professional negotiators ignore such emotions quite readily because, as experience shows, taking up a negotiating position rarely affects 'likeability'. Indeed, it is interesting to note how even the most intense sparring partners sometimes develop quite strong personal bonds away from the negotiating table, notwithstanding the degree of discord that their negotiations may, on occasions, exhibit publicly. The lesson in this observation is that likeability has to do with the *style* you choose to adopt, not the activity itself. (The choice of negotiating style is so important that it has a chapter all to itself – Chapter 3.) For those who fight to protect their own interests, with intelligent, mature application of skill and resolve, the reward is usually *more* respect, not less.

The fear of making a fuss. Many would prefer not to draw attention to themselves, and can see no benefit in doing so. For example, there are many people who hate to complain in a restaurant about poor food, lack of cleanliness, bad service or whatever. If we take this attitude, we rob ourselves of the chance to have matters put right, we lose the opportunity to gain any compensation, and we expose ourselves (or at least other people) to the risk of repeating the same bad experience again. Meanwhile, by refusing to risk embarrassment to ourselves or 'hurting the feelings' of the offending party (in this case the restaurant manager) we also rob him of the chance to improve his business and make amends. On balance, then, 'making a fuss' would appear to be a beneficial action for *all* parties (a win-win situation, in the jargon of negotiating).

4 **The feeling that it is bad manners to attempt to negotiate a better deal.** This inhibition, stemming largely from reluctance to raise the temperature of a discussion to the level of confrontation, is no doubt fostered by the 'let's not make a fuss' tradition of many cultures. This is a common view of outsiders new to negotiating, who see only the press coverage of the public utterances of negotiators – particularly industrial relations negotiators, whose language often appears abrasive and ill-tempered. However, this may only be – and in fact usually is – posturing for public consumption, designed to show the degree of the negotiators' commitment to their case. It is quite understandable that lay people might consider this abusiveness to be the norm of negotiating, but it does not have to be so.

Sometimes it may indeed be a useful tactic to raise the tempo and the temperature of a negotiation session, as we shall see later. Usually, however, this is not the case, and it can be much more beneficial *not* to be confrontational or abrasive. For example, it is hardly realistic to imagine a skilled diplomat or salesman starting off a negotiation by insulting the other parties' parental origin, intelligence or motives: quite the opposite, in fact.

5 **The feeling that if you are open about your position, generous and amenable, surely you will be treated similarly.** This is another fundamental misconception which deters people from negotiating. In fact, more often than not, your position (and perhaps you) will be seen in such circumstances to be weak and malleable. Recognising this fact can be a most powerful motivator, independent of any other, for appreciating that a firm,

'professional' negotiating stance is often necessary, together with a full armoury of skills, however magnanimous you feel yourself to be. Unfortunately, as we have said, people rarely make their best offer first. Unless you challenge them, you will probably always end up with a less favourable outcome than you might have had.

(6) **A natural, human fear of failure:** this is perhaps the most deep-seated reason for reluctance to negotiate, but the solution is simple. Abandon your other inhibitions and misconceptions. Then acquire the relevant skills and practise them, perhaps in role-playing situations (see Chapter 10) or on other occasions when the outcome is not especially important. This way, you can build confidence, which is such an important feature in negotiating better deals.

Clearly the main conclusion to be drawn from the foregoing is **DON'T BE AFRAID TO NEGOTIATE!** It won't make you less likeable or respectable, and done well it will enhance your outcome, whatever the topic for discussion may be.

And yet, many people *still* let their own inhibitions stand in the way of obtaining mutual benefit. Laboratory-based experiments have been conducted which show that some people's reluctance to negotiate can be remarkably strong. Interestingly, women in the western world tend to exhibit this sense of inhibition much more markedly than men, and generally feel the more uncomfortable about negotiating. However, there is no evidence to suggest that women, once actively involved in a negotiation, are any less – or more – able than men.

For those who still feel reluctant to negotiate, perhaps the most convincing argument that negotiation can be worthwhile is to be found in the range of outcomes that are possible if you try – and the number of opportunities that can be missed if you don't.

THE POSSIBILITY OF ENHANCED OUTCOMES

Examples of the benefits that polished negotiating skills can bring are readily apparent if we look at the experiences of many people, with varying skills and aptitudes, who have role-played the same exercises in practice. The different outcomes possible, even though each player starts from the same point, can then be examined. The variations can be astounding.

The first two examples come from standard training courses in negotiating:

case study role play

Insurance. Each party is given a mythical insurance claim. Both parties have weaknesses and strengths in their respective positions, but are only vaguely aware of their opponent's position. They are both given sufficient information to believe that a settlement of around £200,000 would be reasonable, but have been told to get the very best deal possible.

Many teams do indeed settle at around £200,000, but settlements for over £750,000 are regularly won by strong claimants, while strong defendants have escaped with paying £75,000 and less. Quite a difference!

The scale of this difference *can* be even greater. For those parties who are prepared to end in 'deadlock' (i.e., no agreed outcome), offers as low as £15,000 from the defendant, and sums over £1,000,000 demanded by the claimant, are not unknown.

SUMMARY: Insurance Claim

Variations found in practice

DEADLOCK	LOWER SETTLEMENTS	TYPICAL	UPPER SETTLEMENTS	DEADLOCK
£15,000	**below** **£75,000**	around £200,000	**over** **£750,000**	£1,000,000

Note: The difference between the highest and lowest settlements achieved when role-playing is a factor of ten times or more.

House purchases. These exercises are always of interest because

11

so many people go through this experience at some time in their lives (usually with absolutely no training, even though a house will probably be the most expensive purchase they will ever make). Few would ever disagree that buying and selling houses brings out the very worst in people. Negotiating skills are therefore likely to be at a premium here.

In role-playing such a situation, even with quite tight control on what variables will be allowed, settlements regularly take place within a band of plus or minus 20 per cent. Indeed, settlements are very occasionally made well outside what the parties have been told they can afford. A good thing *these* deals are only for practice!

These first two examples from role-playing exercises clearly demonstrate the power of skilful negotiation. If you are interested in engaging in some of these exercises yourself, the details are explained in Chapter 10, under the heading 'Pitfalls and Practice'.

Our final example of what good negotiation can achieve comes from a real situation:

Food supply. Two close neighbours bought some food that had been badly packaged, each of them unaware that the other had done the same. Although the purchase price was very small, both neighbours decided to complain because an element of inherent danger was involved, as well as some personal inconvenience.

One of the purchasers wrote to the manufacturer and suggested a not insignificant sum of monetary compensation which she felt was in order. This was paid.

The other neighbour also wrote a very strong letter of complaint, *but requested no remedial action*. By return came a letter of apology and a replacement of the small item purchased. No payment was made.

Needless to say, when the two neighbours found out what had happened to each other, the second was very upset that she had received no monetary compensation. The lesson, however, was clear to both of them: To gain worthwhile results in a negotiation, you must **make specific proposals – don't just complain!**

Another, broader conclusion, can be drawn from all three of the examples:

MAJOR IMPROVEMENTS IN OUTCOME ARE POSSIBLE,
from the very same starting points in a negotiation, if the appropriate skills are first recognised and then used wisely.

WHO MAKE GOOD NEGOTIATORS?

One of the curious things about negotiating is that acute intelligence on its own is absolutely no guide to a person's likely degree
of talent as a negotiator. What is important is being able to think
quickly on your feet, grasp new points quickly and respond to
them appropriately, all of which is easier if you have a clear
understanding of your opponent's viewpoint, attitudes and
values. (However, you should not be *too* concerned about the
other side's needs, or you may well prejudice your own. You play
your cards, let them play theirs!)

Status in the community or a broad and well-developed
educational background is, like intelligence, no guarantee of
success. Indeed, because of the false sense of an *apparent* power-
base that the possessor of any of these attributes might feel, they
can actually be serious handicaps – particularly if they interfere
with the motivation to negotiate seriously and skilfully. What
will serve you much better is simply to have a full understanding
of the rules and apply the basic skills.

For an excellent example of good negotiators – indeed, natural
negotiators – you will do well to observe children. They generally
show some or all of the following characteristics:

Single-mindedness. They aren't easily distracted from their goal
(although equally-capable negotiating parents know that
distraction is their best chance of dealing with little Johnny who
wants 'just one more sweet').

Persistence. They continue to press their claim long after most of
us would have given up, or at least reconsidered, our initial
demand.

Lack of inhibition. They don't mind making ambitious claims,
even if this creates (for you) an embarrassing situation.

13

Willingness to use sanctions. They are prepared to exploit fully their emotional range: no stiff upper lips and mild sighs of quiet disappointment for them when they are baulked.

Ability to command attention. They are impossible to walk out on, however much you might (occasionally) like to!

Skill at making uncheckable claims. 'I'll scweam and I'll scweam and I'll scweam,' said Violet Elizabeth Bott in the 'William' stories, 'until I'm sick!' I don't think she was sick – but she usually got her own way.

Concern only with the present. Your sanctions therefore appear useless.

Not all negotiators will want to follow the unmodified example of children, for as we have already noted, a high-profile, antagonistic approach can often be counter-productive. However, you may well find the analogy of negotiating with children helpful when negotiating with members of other cultures, such as those described in Chapter 9.

Throughout this book we shall look at the other qualities and skills which distinguish strong and successful negotiators.

Summary

- Negotiation is concerned with resolving conflict, usually by trading concessions. It should not be confused with selling.

- Trust is an important requirement for a successful negotiation, not trickery.

- Skilled negotiators will conclude better deals.

- Negotiating skills can be taught.

- Opportunities abound for negotiating better deals. The first offer is rarely the best.

- Make specific proposals, don't just complain.

- To take advantage of negotiating skills, inhibitions need to be overcome, confidence built, and misconceptions removed.

- Negotiation does not always have to imply confrontation, although it may sometimes require an element of brink-manship.

- The possibilities of enhancing the outcome of a deal can be very substantial. If you ignore these possibilities, you cannot be sure that the other side will. A good deal for *them* may then be struck which will be to *your* disadvantage.

- Don't be afraid to negotiate!

Useful Exercises

- Think of areas where you would *not* wish to negotiate, and then examine why you feel this way. How many reasons relate to your sense of natural justice and trust – and how many to fear? Discuss these reasons with your colleagues. Are your reasons still valid?

- Try a simple role-playing exercise, such as the TRADER in Chapter 10, with a colleague. You will need an umpire to tell each of you the buying-in price, or the maximum resale price, as relevant to the role you play. You may find it is best to ask your umpire to brief each of you in the whole role-play at this stage, as the comments at the end, when read by only one player, will give a grossly unfair advantage! Note that you *must* settle. If necessary, set a deadline of, say, 15 minutes.

- Repeat this last exercise when you have finished the book. What have you learned? (If nothing, how do you feel about trying to negotiate a refund!)

$$\boxed{2}$$

WHEN to NEGOTIATE

To everything there is a season, and a time to every purpose.
Ecclesiastes 2:13

One of the fundamental requirements for success in negotiating better deals is the recognition that opportunities for improving a position exist much of the time, certainly more often than many people would recognise.

It is not just when important contracts are to be negotiated, or major diplomatic or industrial-relations deals are to be done, that negotiating skills can be employed. Every day, even on a personal basis for example, we may have to deal with our family, neighbours, colleagues or officials. As we shall see, even 'non-negotiable' arrangements (such as routine shopping) can sometimes be made negotiable. A key message in Chapter 1 was 'Don't be afraid to negotiate'. This chapter will help you decide when, and when not, to use your negotiating skills.

REQUIREMENTS FOR A NEGOTIATION

When should we consider opening up a negotiation? Usually, the following conditions will apply:

1. **Both parties are willing, in principle, to do a deal.** This indicates that there is at least some common ground. If one party is initially

reluctant to deal, the other party may first have to promote (i.e., sell) the benefits which could arise from their proposals in order to encourage the first party to consider dealing with them. Note, however, that when either side expresses a wish to enter into negotiations, they are signalling that they may have something to give (by way of concessions), as well as something to ask for.

(2) **There is both agreement *and* conflict between the parties.** Otherwise there is little to negotiate. Note that the areas of both agreement and conflict need to be dealt with fully before a settlement can be reached.

(3) **There are variables to trade by way of concessions.** If neither side can find any room for manoeuvre towards a settlement, the negotiation will founder. Searching for the variable items in each side's position is therefore a key requirement for negotiating better deals.

(4) **Both parties have the authority to vary their terms.** Limiting your side's authority to a minimum is, as we shall see, an excellent tactic to enhance the deal you might do, but if there is no authority at all to vary terms then the negotiation becomes pointless or one-sided. Establishing who on the other side has the authority to offer concessions is therefore one of the important tasks to complete in the early exploratory stages of any negotiation.

YOU HAVE CAREFULLY PLANNED YOUR CASE! The great majority of negotiations which promise good results but fail in the end do so because of lack of preparation. If you are not ready to negotiate, you do better to walk away and come back later. Preparation is so important that a full chapter of this book (Chapter 4) is devoted to the subject.

Negotiation may also be appropriate **when something out-of-the-ordinary happens,** such as an extra-large order, the need for exceptional overtime or a special effort, etc. In such circumstances short-term concessions may be made in order to gain a longer-term advantage, for example.

18

LOOKING FOR OPPORTUNITIES

Recalling the comments in the last chapter about the natural inhibitions many people have against making a fuss, you will recognise that part of the difficulty in deciding to negotiate is to overcome the initial embarrassment of rejecting an offer, or claiming a better one. For example, I shall never forget a large dinner party where I sent back a bottle of wine because it was not the year that had been advertised. I received the blackest of disapproving looks from the boss's wife. I later realised that what *she* was drinking was not just the wrong year, but a completely different wine from what she had ordered. But she had made up her mind that she was not going to complain. I still wonder what the wine waiter thought!

It is therefore most instructive to watch how other cultures operate in a bargaining atmosphere. In many Mediterranean countries, the population's propensity for bargaining is almost a cliché, except that the reality is far more impressive (and educational) than any book, film or travelogue would have you believe.

It is not just that, for some cultures, almost anything is negotiable: it is negotiable with tremendous persistence, insistence and fortitude. In part, or perhaps in historical origin, these skills grew out of sheer economic necessity. However, there is no doubt that professional (and social peer-group) pride is also largely responsible for such consistently strong efforts. Consider the example of the Arab traders:

In Paris, it is not unusual to see Moroccans and Tunisians selling leather goods, jewellery and trinkets on the streets. This is a tough way to make a living, for they are highly dependent on their ability to conclude as many deals as possible. In reality, their prices contain a huge negotiating margin, but for someone genuinely interested in buying, these prices are not out of line with those asked elsewhere. (The traders follow one of the key rules of negotiating: they *aim high*.) Nevertheless, if like me you happen to show even a passing interest in their wares, they will be most reluctant to let you go, pursuing you down the street for a considerable distance if necessary. (Another rule they follow: *be persistent*.) If you show any

19

resistance to their 'official' price – which indeed they will expect from even a semi-skilled negotiator – they will parade an astonishing array of offers before you, with invitations to name a price followed by immediate counter-offers, in order to conclude the deal. And conclude a deal they will. The only question is, can you even begin to match their negotiating skills? Few tourists do.

I saw another good example of these skills in practice when, after a visit to the museum in Cairo where Tutankhamun's treasures are stored, my interest was caught by an Arab selling attractive scarab jewellery to tourists. Having spent some time in the city, I soon realised what his other customers did not: his prices were grossly inflated compared with what was easily available elsewhere. I thought, perhaps naïvely, that this was most unfair and so offered, quietly, a fraction of his price. Instead of giving me an angry reception, as I expected, out of the corner of his mouth he made me a counter-offer while continuing to trade at the much higher prices with his other clientele. I was astounded that he could conduct two negotiations, at different levels, simultaneously. Nevertheless, I eventually bought from him, as did the other tourists (at a higher price), and we were all happy.

It is also worth mentioning the responses I have had to these stories when I have related them to other people who travel widely. They all offer similar examples, but many go on to add an ironic twist: when they return to their hotel, they find the shop in the hotel lobby selling the same goods – at prices even lower than they have just negotiated! What is the lesson? Usually that the local hotel shop management was even more adept at negotiating than they were!

Experiences such as these make one wonder what one could achieve at home and in cultures less attuned to bargaining, if one tried harder.

The problem is that we are faced with the *tyranny of the price list*. If we see a price stated, unless it is for a second-hand car or some such item where even our own traditions demand that a counter-offer should be made, we *expect* to have to pay whatever is asked. How many of us, for example, would try as a matter of standard practice to reduce a shop's stated purchase price for a television set, a lawn-mower, a pair of shoes or a shirt? I now try all the time, and have won a better price on *all* these items recently (except for the shirt, where I have failed on three continents! But I still keep trying. . . .)

It is not only the price of a purchase that you should seek to negotiate. Experience shows that many traders are prepared to consider all sorts of proposals which you, as a customer, might make: anything from extending their usual payment terms to free delivery, extended warranties and even spare parts. It does not always work, but it costs nothing to try.

Up until now, you might never have imagined that so many routine purchases could be made negotiable. Once you have built up your confidence and had some success in buying below a published price, however, **you should be able to make substantial savings on your personal purchases, regularly, if only you ask.**

A horrifying thought may now cross your mind: how many opportunities have you let go in the past? From now on, you will no doubt wish to think more confidently, not just about buying and selling more wisely (whether at home or at work), but also about minimising personal bank charges, improving your terms and conditions at work, dealing with awkward colleagues or neighbours, getting the children to bed on time (or even home!) – and accomplishing almost anything else that matters to you.

The important points to remember here are:

- **You have nothing to lose by asking for a better deal**, but you do have to ask! You should not expect to pay the list price for anything as a matter of course. You should not have to be in the position of doing people one-way favours – unless, of course, you want to.

- **You must make specific proposals,** particularly if you are seeking redress for something.

WHEN NOT TO NEGOTIATE

A note of caution should be added here. It may come as a disappointment, but there is another basic fact about negotiating

21

that must not be overlooked in our emphasis on the more positive points:

Negotiating skills cannot give you bargaining power if you have none to start with. If there really is nothing to negotiate, that is if you have nothing to bargain with, there isn't much you can do to improve your position.

Negotiating skills cannot give you power if you have none.

There are also times when there might be plenty to negotiate, at least from the other side's viewpoint, but not to your advantage! At these times, then, don't negotiate if you don't have to.

One of the major negotiating skills is the ability to say 'NO!' If you don't have to discuss concessions, why do so? This is one of the reasons why many salesmen are never allowed to sell outside their price lists. That way, they have to say 'No' to lower offers.

This is the power of *limited authority*. But be careful! It can also be used against you. Skilled buyers, for example, are adept at going to your boss for better deals which you, closer to the customer but with limited authority, might never have offered.

Another occasion when you should not negotiate is when broader objectives might be prejudiced. It is so tempting to go out and 'win a battle', because you think you can gain some short-term advantage for your side, only to find that you have consequently 'lost the war'. This is especially likely when you are emotionally involved in the discussions.

It is particularly difficult to keep an objective overview of your principal aims, and to match your progress against these, when there is every temptation to show that there are *other issues* where you can exercise dominance, even though they are relatively unimportant. It is worth remembering the tale of the eager house-buyer who insisted that an old window-frame be repainted before he agreed to purchase, only to find later that the floor-boards all suffered from dry rot: a definite case of mistaken priorities.

Finally, there is one more situation when it is best to avoid entering into a negotiation, one which we have already mentioned: i.e., When you are not prepared. Many are the salesmen, for example, who thought they had a deal sewn up but then lost it at the last fence because they were too confident to prepare properly.

One of the most common reasons people suffer the embarrassing consequences of incomplete preparation is simply failure to consult their own side adequately, in advance. There is nothing worse than being undermined, or overruled, by your own side *after* you think you have struck a wonderful bargain.

Another common reason for inadequate preparation is lack of time, resulting in pressure for quick dealing. Pressure of time can be a useful asset in cutting out wasteful, unproductive argument, but it can also be used most powerfully against you. All too often businesses have made unsatisfactory purchases, for example, because their buyers were under pressure to do a deal quickly. If you want your purchasing team to buy well, they must be given time to build up their power base, to establish their negotiating posture, and generally to weave their magic in the market place.

Summary

- More often than you may realise, there is a better deal to be obtained. But you will almost certainly have to ask for it.

- Don't just complain. Make specific proposals.

- Aim high with these proposals, and be persistent.

- Watch other people negotiating, and learn from them.

- Don't negotiate when you have nothing to bargain with, or when broader objectives might be prejudiced.

- Successful negotiations need to be well prepared and planned.

- Don't be caught ill-prepared by having to do quick deals.

Useful Exercises

- Remind yourself: What are the usual conditions for a negotiation? When is it best *not* to negotiate?

- Reflect on all the occasions you can remember in the past when you now realise you *could* have negotiated for a better deal, but didn't. If you have the courage, make a short list of them and analyse what it was that stopped you from doing better.

- Reward yourself the next time a similar situation occurs in which you do achieve a better deal.

STYLE

'Tous les genres sont bons, hors le genre ennuyeux'
(All styles are good, except for the tiresome sort.)
Voltaire, *L'Enfant Prodigue*

Your choice of the style or manner in which to conduct a negotiation is a major element in winning better bargains. The decision as to which style is likely to be the most appropriate is a basic part of preparation. It is so important that it is worth consideration in its own right.

There are two fundamental choices:

A cooperative style, which aims to ensure that *both* parties should gain some benefit. This is therefore a *win-win* style of negotiation.

A competitive style, which is designed to maximise only *one* side's advantage, at a specific cost to the other. This is clearly a much more aggressive stance and is therefore a *win-lose* style of negotiation.

Deciding which style to adopt is not just a matter of personal preference. As any negotiation will involve at least two parties, your choice of style must take into account your opponent's probable choice. This will almost certainly affect your own position – and a broad variety of permutations is possible.

PERMUTATIONS OF STYLE

Consider the extremes of opponents' styles which you are likely to meet: some won't even require a negotiating posture from you; others won't allow one. The range of possibilities is as follows:

If your opponent makes an **immutable demand** upon you, which is genuinely inflexible – or at least you believe it is – you have no option but to accede (i.e., simply surrender in a defenceless collapse) or to refuse the demand. If you refuse, but the demand persists, you are effectively in a state of 'warfare'. If you happen to be a diplomat, this may possibly be literally true, but for most of us this is hopefully only a figurative term! More usually, you will be in a state of debate, which might become quite heated if the demand persists and continues to be immutable. Note that this is *not* negotiation because for that to take place, the demand must be stated with some flexibility, allowing concessions to be traded.

If, however, a **straightforward offer** is made, for example an offer to buy or sell, you can choose either to accept (by which the deal is done) or to refuse. If the refusal is accepted at face value, that too makes an end of the matter.

Neither of the above possibilities involves negotiating. However, the second possibility can be turned into an occasion for negotiation in two ways: If you don't like the initial offer, you can either induce the other party to amend the offer or you can make a counter-proposal. Deciding which of these options you should take is part of your planning deliberations. Do you make the running by offering a counter-proposal, or are you in a stronger position? Can you persuade the other party to withdraw the first offer and replace it with something even more attractive, with no concession from your side?

Either way, you are at least now involved in a negotiation.

As an alternative scenario, you might receive a **conditional offer**: 'If you will do this, I can give you that.' If you accept the conditions, you have given a (conditional) acceptance. However, remembering that the first offer is rarely the best, you would probably respond with a counter-proposal and, again, you are now in a negotiating position.

The best option for you, of course, would be a **straightforward donation**, which presumably you would accept – there being no strings attached – as a charitable offer. (In this case, you do not need a book on how to negotiate better deals!)

All of the foregoing is summarized in the following table:

SUMMARY OF POSSIBILITIES

Style	Action by Party A	Reaction by Party B		Outcome
Battle	Immutable demand	Acceptance	=	Defenceless collapse
		or		
		Refusal	=	Warfare or debate
Sale or Purchase	Straight offer	Straight acceptance	=	Purchase or sale
		or		
		Counter proposal	=	Negotiation
		or		
		Refusal	=	No deal
Negotiation	Conditional offer	Conditional acceptance	=	Conditional settlement
		or		
		Counter proposal	=	Negotiation
Charitable Offer	Donation	Acceptance	=	Charitable gifts

The point of the table above is to emphasize, first, that you won't always be in a negotiating situation, and second, that you can often determine whether or not negotiation takes place by being prepared for your opponent's style and then adopting an appropriate style of response.

You can see from all of this that the options vary from neither party obtaining any benefit, i.e., a *lose-lose* situation, to both parties sharing benefits as the result of a *win-win* or cooperative approach. In between these, there might also be *deadlock*, where any possible outcome is held in abeyance, or *win-lose* negotiating – the competitive approach by which one party does well, but at the expense of the opponent, who either comes out of the negotiation badly or at least not as well. (Note that in this terminology, a 'loss' may not be a real loss, but just a failure to gain from a *possible* benefit. We refer to this in more detail under 'Game Theory'.)

These varieties of negotiating possibilities can be summarised by the following table:

WHO WINS?

Event	Result	Environment
The Cold War	LOSE – LOSE	Paranoia, distrust, etc.
Battle	Uncertainty	Hostile, heated debate
Inflexibility	– DEADLOCK –	Incompatible demands, stubborn resolve
Competitive negotiation	WIN – LOSE	Aggression, conflict
Cooperative negotiation	WIN – WIN	Non-combative sharing, mutual understanding

Let's look at the results of these possibilities in some detail, starting with those which offer the least reward, as set out above in descending order.

LOSE-LOSE SITUATIONS

At the start of this book, we suggested that negotiations do not have to be confrontational. A cold war clearly is just that, and rarely provides a beneficial outcome to either party. Nearly always it will produce a lose-lose result. Note that a loss in this context may only mean that neither side makes any gains, which could have been achieved if they had only started out more positively. It could also, of course, mean that both sides will actually end up worse off than when they started.

If a shared loss produces only such fruitless outcomes, why then does it happen so often?

The only useful and valid reason for indulging in lose-lose tactics is to create a power-base. This is a rather subtle activity, where a short-term gain is passed over in order to win some longer-term, strategic advantage. (We look at this further in Chapter 8.) However, by far the most frequent reason is that both of the negotiating parties are relatively unskilled.

Thus a more typical example of a lose-lose situation is when a hungry supplier, with a good product, asks for more advantage than his buyer is able (or is prepared) to give, despite there being a real need. The seller loses the deal and the buyer is forced to make an inferior purchase elsewhere. Both parties lose out. It is rather like the case of the spoilt child who won't let a friend play with a favourite toy, despite knowing that an angry parent will then take the toy away and neither child will be able to play with it.

Similar situations arise in industrial relations disputes when the unrealistic ambitions of a work-force for better conditions, the intransigence of the management, or both, result in strike action. The work force loses pay, the management can't satisfy customer demand and both sides lose job-security, because the business is weakened as other suppliers take over its work. These, sadly, are situations that continue to repeat themselves.

The short-sighted nature of some negotiators is reminiscent of the following surrealist story, which has a very direct moral:

Very late one night, a motorist runs out of petrol in the middle of some very desolate countryside. Fortunately, far away, the motorist spies the light of a farmhouse. He has an empty can in his car, so he sets off hopefully, thinking that the farmer is bound to let him have some petrol. This will be enough to get him to the nearest village, where he can stay the night and fill up in the morning. 'What good luck!' the motorist thinks to himself.

The walk up the mountainside to the farm is tough and gruelling. As the subject of our story sets off, he starts to feel the

31

biting wind and driving rain. Soon, he is exhausted, cold and soaked to the skin. Then he tears his trousers on some brambles. Thoroughly demoralised, he begins to wonder what the farmer is like.

'Perhaps he will be very bad-tempered', the driver thinks to himself. 'The farmer might think I am about to steal his sheep or burgle his house. He certainly won't be pleased to be disturbed by a stranger, this late at night.'

Just then, the lights go out in the farm-house. The farmer has obviously gone to bed.

'Oh, dear!' the motorist mutters to himself. 'Anyone would be furious to be woken up on a night like this, especially a farmer who probably has to be up at the crack of dawn tomorrow. If he answers at all, he'll probably thrust a shot-gun out of the window and threaten violence. Miserable old fool! Just what you would expect from people who live round here.'

Just then, the motorist arrives at the farmhouse and knocks on the door. He just can't imagine the farmer wanting to come out and help him on a night like this. And he certainly isn't going to stand around and be abused. Suddenly, the farmer opens up a bedroom window and shouts out, 'Who's there?'

The stranded motorist shouts back, 'You can keep your bloody petrol, if that's your attitude!'

Think the worst of people, and you will probably prove yourself right. If you think you aren't going to like 'southerners' (or 'northerners', as the case may be), you will probably be right. If you convince yourself that you haven't a hope of pushing your next price-rise through, you probably won't. As sales-trainers never tire of telling their students, it is all a matter of having the right mental attitude. As with selling, so it is with life in general.

Those conversant with transactional analysis will be familiar with the importance of maintaining an 'adult' mental attitude. In our context, this can be described as being well-balanced, unemotional and factual. In the face of outrageous provocation, whether 'child-like', emotive and immature ('I'll take my bat and ball away if you won't let me play') or 'parental,' judgemental and bossy ('Don't you speak to me like that'), it is essential *not* to be tempted into giving

32

equally childish or parent-like responses. By answering unhelpful stimuli with either type of 'non-adult' responses, we multiply the risks of creating a lose-lose situation every time.

In summary, therefore, the key to avoiding this is to maintain your position as an 'adult', whether as the stimulator (initiator) of the discussion or as the respondent, *whatever* the style your opponent adopts. Graphically, it looks like this:

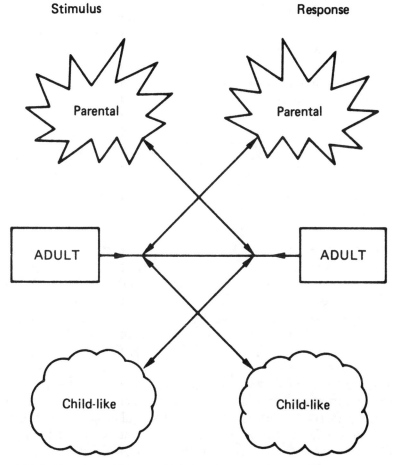

Adapted from *I'm OK – You're OK.* Courtesy of the author, Dr Thomas A. Harris.

This aspect of interpersonal relationships of course affects everything we do. When coupled with other skills, such as assertiveness, an adult approach can help to enrich all our lives. It can help us, for example, towards these important goals:

Being able to say 'No', comfortably. This is as important in everyday situations as it is when negotiating.

Being able to express our feelings, with confidence, about matters which we dislike and would like to change.

Building positive and fruitful relationships with others.

Enhancing our own self-esteem (and the esteem in which we are held by others).

Being able to say 'NO', comfortably, is important.

34

Those who claim to be experts in transactional analysis and assertiveness are inclined to disapprove of simplifications of the issues briefly touched upon above, which are indeed worth further study. There are many excellent books on these subjects. Suffice to say here that these skills form a major part of strong and successful negotiating. In particular, they are especially relevant in preventing lose-lose situations, which are, as we have seen, clearly to be avoided.

BATTLES

In Figure 2, we indicated that a cold war can lead to a lose-lose outcome. Sometimes this can be avoided by building up strong personal relationships and trust. The cold war can, however, degenerate into a 'hot war', or battle. The eventual outcome might still be lose-lose, Deadlock (see later) or even win-lose. If you are very lucky, you might even convert this to a shared win-win, but there will always be some doubt about the outcome because a feature of any battle is uncertainty and a loss of stability.

This aspect of destabilisation sometimes makes battle an attractive tactic to some negotiators, especially when their case is inherently weak. It is used with the direct intention of putting you off your stride. If despite all your interpersonal skills, as well as cool assertiveness and, perhaps, the benefits of Transactional Analysis, you still find yourself in a battle, you need to adopt a style that is going to be appropriate. Battles usually leave little room for social niceties.

Note also that those who regularly adopt destabilising battle-tactics are usually well practised fighters, accustomed to getting their own way with this approach. For them, fighting a battle is like playing on home ground; this is what they know best. If you are not an equally skilled and practised fighter, you are well advised to steer clear of this arena.

In such situations, it is therefore especially important not to be provoked; you must develop a tough skin. It is also important to develop a strong power-base if you can, or at least a strong defence. Beware, however: experience shows that preparing for battle can increase the likelihood of being in one, so watch carefully that you are not yourself giving out fighting stimuli.

How to defend against a battle

- Develop a strong power base (or, at least, a strong defence).

- Exhibit rock-solid confidence.

- Keep a balanced and detached view.

- Keep control of what you are prepared to discuss, how, and in what order.

- Monitor carefully the pace and atmosphere of the discussion. Be prepared to redirect it, if necessary.

- Avoid initially either an aggressive stance or for that matter a defensive one. Both can be the sort of fighting stimuli referred to above.

- If you find yourself on difficult ground, be prepared to be flexible by changing either the topic (preferably across a broad front) or the tactics.

Note especially that a fast pace can very quickly accelerate out of either party's control. It is for this reason that it is important not to be too sensitive to barbed comments, but to stay calm and try to appear ultra-reasonable, ready to be conciliatory and coop-erative as a reward for any change in the aggressive posture of your opponent.

If this opening style does not mollify your opponent and deflect the attack, it is then vital, at an early stage, to be prepared to counter-attack.

Finally, it is also necessary to be prepared to walk out of the discussion. *Arguments* on their own cannot be negotiated; only *proposals* can.

DEADLOCK

Deadlock is worth examining on its own, because it might arise not only out of a battle, but also during quite unemotional discussion or negotiation when both parties are reluctant to move towards each other beyond a certain limit.

Deadlock is very different from both lose-lose and battle situations because the end-result is *intentionally held in suspense.* Unlike the other two styles, deadlock may allow the final outcome to be enhanced from your point of view. With lose-lose in particular, this clearly cannot happen.

In other words, deadlock is brinkmanship played to the limit, where both parties are aiming for a larger slice of the cake: i.e., win-lose negotiating. The experienced negotiator may appear to be driving you into the ground, but unlike the fighter, he (or she) is usually too skilled to overdo things and thus lose benefits – by you walking out, for example. For this reason, a threat to do just that is an especially powerful tool. (But make sure that it isn't you who will be the net loser!)

Deadlock is especially interesting because it can be a natural outcome of both parties applying two of the basic negotiating rules which will be covered later, in more detail:

1) **The party which offers the first concessions will usually be the less successful.**

2) **The more successful party will usually be the one with the highest aspirations.**

A special feature of deadlock therefore is that, unlike lose-lose and battles, it most often results when *skilled* negotiators meet, with very high (but conflicting) aspirations. The question is really who will crack first. Both parties will have concessions to give (or else it is not a negotiation, but simply a battle). The problem is just that neither party wants to make the first offer.

This naturally is not a comfortable situation to be in, but in order to handle it well, it is important to come to terms with it. Some people like to suggest that you should approach deadlock with the view that you cannot expect to win every time, so relax and enjoy it! Of that advice, the most valid part is that you should certainly not become over-tense. Many negotiators therefore like to practice deep-breathing routines and other exercises to promote physical relaxation. These are not skills that are easily acquired, but they are beneficial. For this reason, many international athletes use the same techniques before a big event, and you might like to consider doing the same.

It is equally helpful to remember that while the situation may be uncomfortable for you, your opponent will probably be feeling the same way. Not everyone will feel the pressure to the same degree, however, and practice helps to keep it under control. This is where role playing exercises beforehand can be of special assistance. Don't shy away from getting into a deadlock, though, when it is appropriate. Deadlock can be a very useful tactic to enhance the outcome, if used properly.

If you are going to be prepared for deadlock, there are some important rules to keep in mind:

Don't provoke. This can mean refraining from increasing the level of activity that might be under dispute, not going back over old disputes, and not publicising your position to a third party in the hope of getting extra leverage.

Do question. What areas *are* open for negotiation? What suggestions do the other side have to advance? What exactly is the foundation for *their* case?

Seek new variables. What else can be offered for discussion with regard to concessions? e.g., price, terms of payment, delivery, specifications, guarantees, packaging, follow-on business, future behaviour, etc.

Be positive. Concentrate on how things can be improved this time, for example, not what went wrong last time.

Don't interrupt, and do listen carefully. The art of giving and picking up signals will be covered later, but it is surprising how many negotiations founder because signals are missed.

If you find yourself in a deadlock and want to start taking positive steps to break it, consider the following possibilities:

Make an offer that both sides should agree to put the matter in abeyance, and move on, in order that progress can be made.

Create a diversion. Consider a change of emphasis, location, or even personnel (especially the team-members who have had the most of the face-to-face contact so far).

Make an offer of an unwanted concession, reluctantly.

Suggest a trade-off of a concession already agreed.

Propose a recess to cool down and reconsider the position, highlighting the areas to be resolved. Then:

Restate and clarify both their position and yours, in terms of what areas of common ground exist and what are the matters standing in the way of progress.

Trade minor concessions for a major move in your favour.

Finally, consider the following actions:

Issue a deadline. Give warnings that you are going to do this and try to have some significant offer or proposal up your sleeve, which might break the deadlock, to offer in exchange for something of value to you.

Get them to put their cards on the table. How keen are they, really, to do a deal and settle? What is their most important concern, and what is less important?

If helpful, remove the deadline.

Propose going to arbitration (or in industrial relations disputes, a professional conciliation service).

ARGUING

Whether you are in a battle or a deadlock, it is especially important that you obey the rules of good argument; otherwise you will be in danger of losing control. These rules are as follows:

Make only a few points at a time. The great temptation in making your case is to flood the other side with all the points in your favour that you can think of. Choose just one or two of your strongest, best-supported arguments and then shut up. Weaker points will only dilute your case. You can make the other points later, if you need to, as further reinforcement of your views.

Build up a case, logically and carefully, before drawing the inevitable conclusion that you disagree with the other side. Don't say you disagree first, and *then* explain why. This will only alert the other side and encourage them to fight you on each and every point you make. Rather, explain how you see the position, draw the inevitable conclusions that you feel must therefore be made, and *then* say you must disagree.

Listen carefully. It is difficult to listen when speaking. Don't interrupt. Furthermore, try to avoid point-scoring, clever or personal remarks, allocating blame, issuing wild threats and any other non-adult ploys. Such tactics rarely help to produce a positive outcome, and might also be remembered with a grudge next time you need to negotiate with your present opponent.

Seek clarification of the other side's position by neutral summaries and questions, e.g., 'I believe your key points are . . .' or 'So what you are saying is . . ., is that right?' or 'Does that mean . . .?' or 'What do you want us to understand when you say . . .?' It is a very powerful tactic to restate an opponent's case. This shows you have understood it, and forms a useful base for:

Demand justification of the opposing case, point by point (in a neutral manner, or else you will appear to be point-scoring) by asking 'Why do you claim . . .?' 'What is your reason for . . .?' etc.

Check out priorities. What are the most important points for the other party – and which are the least important? This is necessary in any negotiation so that you can gauge both the cost to you of whatever concessions you may have to offer, and their value to the other side.

Be positive. This means being assertive about your case, certainly, but it also means refraining from out-of-hand dismissal of any points that might be made by your opponent before they have been fully developed. Being positive also means indicating your willingness to seek a realistic outcome.

GAME THEORY

Win-win and win-lose are the most likely style for the majority of negotiations because, as we have already seen, one of the requirements for a genuine negotiation, carried out in good faith, is that both parties do indeed wish to settle.

The choice of negotiating style which produces the best result has been analysed in game theory. In brief, the individual party who wins the most is the one who successfully wins a competitive win-lose negotiation. However, the total benefit is greatest for *both* sides when a *win-win* outcome is sought.

In a caring, sharing world, the win-win or cooperative style would surely be the mature choice. The problem, however, is that in our world not all parties will necessarily care what benefit *you* may obtain; nor will they always want to share what *they* might gain.

With these thoughts in mind, the practical approach to the choice of negotiating style, arising from game theory, is as follows:

The Game Theory Solution to Negotiating

- Seek a win-win outcome whenever you can, so that both sides can obtain the greatest benefit.

- However, if the other side should attempt to go for what we have described as a win-lose outcome, you should also revert to an aggressive, competitive, win-lose approach.

The second part of this solution is designed to protect your own case, which will clearly be threatened if you continue in a cooperative spirit in the face of a competitive assault.

It should also be used to penalise the other side for being uncooperative. As with Pavlov's dogs, only 'good' behaviour should be rewarded!

Before looking at both win-lose and win-win negotiations in more detail, there is one other noteworthy consideration which arises from the more theoretical aspects of the way we define a 'loss'.

We have chosen to define a loss, in all our discussions on the practicalities of negotiations, as an unrealised gain – which is not necessarily an *actual* loss.

41

Now, in Chapter 1 we said that no party to a negotiation should end up in a worse position than when they started, unless they were incompetent or the other side were dishonest. This statement is an important one to make, but it is based on a theoretical definition of loss which is rather different from the one we are using now, for example in describing win-lose negotiations.

Let's consider what the situation would be if a supplier should seek a unilateral price rise, or a customer should seek a unilateral price reduction. The degree of price movement may be negotiated, but if *any* ground is conceded without some benefit in return, surely that side will have sustained a genuine loss, in that they will then be worse off than when they started?

The answer is 'no' in theory, even though it is 'yes' in practice. This paradox might best be explained with an analogy, which we will call 'The Farmer's Complaint'. It runs as follows:

When a harvest is less than a farmer might have hoped for, because of poor weather conditions perhaps, it is traditional for a farmer anywhere in the world to complain that he has actually sustained a loss. In theory, he has not. The farmer may not have been able to sell as much as he would have liked, and he may therefore have sustained a net *financial* loss, but he will not have had a net *crop* loss. In other words, he started with no crop and ended with less than he expected, but he is not actually left with less crop than when he started.

Now let's look again at our example of a unilateral price rise. The buyer may indeed now be financially worse off, but he or she did have a free choice. The buyer was not forced to continue to deal with that supplier. Equally, if a customer were to enforce a price reduction, the seller can then decline to supply. As far as theory is concerned, a loss is not sustained because the starting point should be regarded as the stage *before* the supplier was selling to the buyer, i.e., before the two sides were trading together.

So much for the theory. In our terms, there has been a win-lose negotiation. Although the supplier (in the case where the customer enforced a price reduction) may still choose to keep the business at 'worse' (lower) prices, the supplier *has* lost some of the original profit from the business – profit which he had before the new prices were 'forced' upon him – and the *customer*, in this example, has therefore 'won' the negotiation.

COMPETITIVE (OR WIN-LOSE) NEGOTIATION

This is sometimes called *distributive* negotiation, because the issue is seen as a cake of fixed size, and the negotiation is to establish how the cake will be divided up, or distributed. Inevitably, one side's gain is the other's loss, so it is a power struggle with high stakes. This is clearly an advantageous style to adopt if you have a strong power-base, no concern with achieving an 'equitable' settlement as long as you get what *you* want, and no regard for downstream consequences (such as what might happen in a subsequent negotiation, when the tables could be turned and you could find yourself in a weak instead of a strong position).

A more detailed look at power, and its cousins, aspiration and skill, will come later (Chapter 8), as they are important considerations in their own right. However, suffice it to say here that not only is the true strength of your power-base important, *but also what your opponent believes it to be.* As in the field of advertising, so with negotiation. What people *believe* to be the truth is more important in determining how they will act in a negotiation than the *real* truth. As the advertising professionals say (well, some of them), 'perception *is* reality.'

If you decide at the outset to go for a win-lose negotiation, here are the steps you should follow:

Actions for a Win-Lose Negotiation

- Make quite clear your absolute commitment to what you must have.
- State what the consequences will be if you don't get it.

- Try to prevent your opponents from specifying their commitments. If they do,

- Provide some form of face-saving exit for them – perhaps by offering a mollifying concession which costs you little.

Throughout this type of negotiation especially, your aim must be to persuade your opponent that the best outcome you could expect is actually the *least* you can possibly accept. However, because it is a negotiation and not a battle, you will need to exchange concessions.

Your skill comes in releasing small concessions, in return for bigger ones, slowly and painfully. The best style to adopt here is to reward concessions given, with smaller ones, rather than be completely intransigent and risk the other party walking away, thus putting you in a lose-lose position.

Skilled negotiators will prefer to play the strong, silent type and let the other side do the talking, the explaining, and then the offering. When the other side is faced with silence, rather than return the same they will usually want to fill the silence with words, which quickly become concessions. This is illustrated by the following scenario:

Salesman, smiling:
   'We hope you find our bid to be attractive'.
The buyer is silent. There is a pregnant pause. The salesman wonders what he has got wrong. He tries again, as engagingly as he can:
   'Well, we know we have competition, but we believe our offer should be very well placed'.
This is met with more silence. Becoming somewhat alarmed now, the salesman offers an inducement:
   'Well, suppose we considered a small rebate. How would you feel if we gave you 2½% if you took the whole volume we have tendered for?'
Mr Strong-and-Silent Buyer still says nothing, but frowns and gives an imperceptible shake of the head. The Salesman, desperate now, sweetens the deal:
   'I suppose I could go up to 5%, but I'd need an order today'.
More silence . . . and so it goes on until the Buyer is satisfied that he has won the best deal possible.

The poor salesman in the above case is doing exactly what he has been told to do: 'Don't lose the business' and (as befits all good negotiators) 'Trade concessions for some reciprocal benefit.' In the first offer, the rebate was linked to getting the whole order. In the second, the increased rebate was linked to obtaining an immediate commitment. The problem was that the salesman just couldn't bring himself to sit tight and let the buyer be the one to break the silences. He should have asked direct questions and insisted upon a response at the very beginning. (We look further at dealing with 'difficult' characters in Chapter 9, and at similar negotiating ploys in Chapter 10.)

How to Defend against Win-Lose Tactics

- Take up an equally strong position. Dig in early and present clear, but unemotional, opposition. Then:

- Seek an exchange of information to clarify each party's position.

- Establish why each party holds its respective position.

- Stress the consequences to *the other party* of a failure to resolve the issue.

The intention of this procedure is to enhance mutual respect, while indicating quite clearly the predicament both parties will be in if agreement is not possible. Then, try to set up a shared problem-solving approach, with the intention of moving the other party toward a win-win rather than a win-lose solution.

COOPERATIVE (OR WIN-WIN) NEGOTIATION

In this situation the two parties work together in search of the best settlement possible for both sides, so it is sometimes styled an *integrative* negotiation. Each party will, of course, wish to protect their own side's interests, but the style will be that of a joint problem-solving exercise rather than that of an adversarial fight to get the largest slice of whatever is at issue. As a consequence, in the early stages much more time will be spent in identifying the problem areas and looking, together, for solutions.

In order to get the best outcome, the opposing parties may wish to share information in order to move to a position of mutual trust. Both need to be sure, of course, that what they are being told is indeed true. It is partly for this reason that cooperative deals will most readily be struck where both parties share some common ground and have some affinity for each other.

This establishment of mutual trust is a major feature of successful win-win deals. You may well feel that the following quotation is appropriate here: 'Politeness and humility are important. If you are humble, the other person finds it easier to communicate with you, and communication is the essence of good business.' (Ranjit Sethia)

Where one party is weaker, that side will probably be the one to make most of the running, establishing what the other side's problems are and ranking them in order of importance. They will also have to work harder at getting the other side to be equally open, perhaps by volunteering sensitive information first as an expression of good-will.

Actions for a Win-Win Negotiation

- Signal clearly that your intentions are for a win-win outcome (and seek confirmation of this from the other side).

- Identify problems, initially, rather than solutions.

- Establish an atmosphere of mutual respect and trust. This may often best be achieved if you:

- Tackle those problems with the greatest potential for a win-win outcome first, especially if they are difficult, so that a good head of steam can be generated towards resolving subsequent issues the same way.

46

- Share information, in equal measures, step by step. Even if this sharing is not reciprocated initially, it should be continued, cautiously, for a short while.

- Reward positive signals from the other side. Note that research shows that it is the regular frequency of concessions that is conducive to cooperative bargaining, not the size.

- Avoid a defensive posture. Be amenable as long as the climate is favourable.

- Avoid a 'legalistic' or contractual approach, if possible.

Choosing whether to start with a win-lose or a win-win style is an important part of preparing for a negotiation. We will look at the options more closely in the next chapter.

Reward positive signals.

QUALITIES REQUIRED OF NEGOTIATORS

Before leaving the broad subject of style, it is worth commenting further on the personal qualities required of professional negotiators.

In general, independent of what is being negotiated, they:

say nothing, or at least as little as possible.

listen carefully and are not overtly aggressive.

talk knowledgeably and confidently, in strong, positive pictures (when they do talk).

are shrewd even if they don't choose to show it!

have ambitious goals.

NEVER concede without gaining an advantage in return.

concede slowly, with limited authority.

look for inexpensive concessions to trade for valuable ones.

have influence and the ability to use it.

have credibility and respect from the other side, regarding both what they stand for and what they have to say. This is clearly best built up by demonstrating personal integrity and establishing good relations with the other side over 'good' times as well as 'bad', if at all possible.

have empathy for others, i.e., constant awareness of the effect they (and their team) have on their opponents and other interested parties.

have agile minds and a capacity for sustained concentration. This is clearly important because however well-planned your negotiation is, you will have to think quickly on your feet and keep all the balls in the air. Since you must not be channelled into what may become an unprofitable cul-de-sac, this agility of mind is especially important in order to handle specific items, as necessary, while still exploring across a broad front.

have the ability to think clearly under stress. If you can see the stress points coming, you will be at an advantage, because pre-emptive anticipation will reduce the stress.

Then, finally, there are 'the four Ps', the key words which will describe any skilled and successful negotiator in action:

POSITIVE

PATIENT

PLACID

PREPARED

Summary

- You do not always have to negotiate for an acceptable settlement. (If you are lucky, the deal you want may be *given* to you.)

- Lose-lose situations are to be avoided, but deadlock can be a very useful tool for getting the best deal.

- Negotiation can be either win-lose (competitive) or win-win (cooperative).

- Win-lose, being competitive, may be preferable where you know for sure that you can win a power struggle.

- Win-win, being cooperative, requires *both* sides to negotiate with this style if the outcome is to be successful. It will, however, produce the best over-all result, if both parties want it.

- A win-lose attempt against you must be resisted and, if possible, penalised, to protect future negotiations.

- Win-lose may be turned into win-win by taking a strong position, stressing the consequences of failure to agree, and then seeking to solve problems together with the other side.

- Mutual respect and trust are fundamental requirements, especially with a win-win strategy.

- Make your highest expectations sound like they are the *least* you can accept, especially if using a win-lose strategy.

- The style of a negotiation will depend in part on the qualities and skills of the parties involved.

Useful Exercises

- Remind yourself: what are the requirements for success if you choose to play for the highest stakes, and go for a win-lose negotiation?

- Likewise, how do you convert a win-lose attempt by the other side into a win-win?

- Think of negotiations you have been in, in the past. Were they win-win or win-lose? How did you feel about the outcome?

  If they were win-lose, what was the style of the other side initially? If you were on the losing side, what could you have done about it? If you won, did you get the best possible result?

  If they were win-win, how could you have done better?

- Practise arguing professionally. Listen to others arguing and note what they do well, and what they do wrong. Learn from them.

- Start to analyse people's comments to you as Adult, Child-like or Parental. Monitor your responses similarly.

Where's
my

─ What
a) simple

| P R E Y |

Who to include
in tea
─ what time

Why?   Who?   What   When   How   How   What   What
       my   obj   should high much order
       with   we h.

4

PREPARATION

Qui desiderat pacem, praeparet bellum' Vegetius, De Re Bellum.
(Let him who desires peace, prepare for war.)

Sound planning and careful preparation are vital for a successful negotiation. It is so easy to presume beforehand that all will go well; that there will be no unpleasant surprises and everything will run smoothly. Such presumptions are rarely warranted, and then only when the preparation has been meticulous. It is an awful cliché that 'to fail to plan is to plan to fail', but it is inescapably true. It is not only very lazy to wait until the meeting to 'see what they have to say', it is also very bad tactics. Basic planning should NOT be done while negotiating.

In the last chapter, the choices of style available to both parties were discussed. We shall now look at the planning required for any specific negotiation, including the very important factors of style and general negotiating climate.

Overall, we need to ask ourselves the following questions:

Why are we entering into a negotiation, and what will it really be about?

Who will we be negotiating with? What will be *their* style and range of objectives?

What are our objectives? How are they to be valued, and in what order of importance are they to be ranked?

When will suit us best to hold the negotiations? And when would *not*?

How should we negotiate? What should be our choice of style? Will it be more appropriate to aim for a win-lose competitive outcome, or a cooperative win-win approach?

How high should we pitch our initial demands? To what degree should we be prepared to modify these demands each time we are faced with counter-offers?

What variables in our position are we prepared to exchange as concessions in return for any counter-offers? What are we *not* prepared to exchange?

What order should we set for offering our concessions, and what else might we be prepared to include?

Who do we need to include in our team, and what will their respective roles be?

Where do we want the negotiations to take place? Do we want to meet on our ground, theirs, or on neutral territory?

How much time will we need to reserve?

What assumptions have we made in our planning? How can we check their validity?

The careful planner will have answered these questions well before a negotiation begins.

THE WHY, WHO, WHAT AND WHEN OF NEGOTIATION

Why do you need to negotiate? You might be seeking to improve your position, or to preserve it, or to protect it against some threat or opposition. Do make sure that you consider all the circumstances, however. It could be that you *don't* need to negotiate at all.

We saw in Chapter 1 that negotiation is about the resolution of conflict, usually by the exchange of concessions. If you see no conflict, or you have nothing to concede, then there is nothing to negotiate. Before you take such a view, however, establish what the *other* side's position might be. You might find that you *are* in conflict after all. Alternatively, there may well be concessions that you *should* be prepared to make, against your initial judgement perhaps, for a longer-term objective that you had not originally recognised in the first analysis.

Equally, there might be all the right circumstances for a negotiation in theory, but as we saw in Chapter 2, it may not be to your advantage to engage in debating those particular subjects. For example, there might be bigger issues to consider. Don't let your enthusiasm for sitting down at the negotiating table to debate one specific point over-balance the requirements of the broader picture. Sometimes it may be judicious to avoid negotiating lesser issues in order to keep your powder dry for more important ones.

Let us assume, however, that after your review of both sides' position you *do* want to negotiate. You now need to know *who* you are going to have to negotiate with – and what style they are likely to adopt. (Chapter 9 will discuss personality and cultural differences in some detail, in order to provide additional help on this subject.)

Remember that it is very important to identify early on who is the decision-maker on the opposing team. In some Oriental and Eastern European cultures, especially, it is not unusual to find that the eventual decision-maker is not part of the team, so you will require extra reserves of patience while that person (or persons) is consulted.

In the Western world it is more usual for at least one member of the team to be empowered to make decisions. You need to identify who this person is – during your planning deliberations if at all possible. It will also be very important during the negotiations to monitor carefully the reactions of this decision-maker, in particular, to your proposals. To help you here, it is therefore often a very good tactic to ask, tactfully, at the beginning of the negotiation: 'If we reach agreement to-day, does anyone else need to be involved to sign?' If the answer is 'Yes', or prevarication, establish who does have

'In some cultures, it is not unusual to find that the eventual decision maker is not part of the team.'

decision-making authority and ask whether it is possible for that person to join you.

If the decision-maker cannot or will not join you, consider reducing the scale of your *own* team's authority.

In organising your planning, much of your time will be devoted to deciding *what* are you most keen to negotiate for, and what are the subsidiary considerations. Once you are in the heat of a complicated negotiation, it is all too easy to find yourself winning on the smaller issues but losing on your main objective.

For this reason, it is essential to take these two steps beforehand:

Formalise *your* objectives in terms of priorities. Consider all of them. What do you want most, and what is it worth to you? Does your own side's hierarchy agree with you? You don't want to find that your objectives have been changed by your superiors for you in mid-negotiation!

Establish what *their* objectives and priorities might be, as best you can. How much are these worth to them, and how much might they cost you if you have to make significant concessions? Obviously, you will want to trade the concessions that are of least cost to you and maximum benefit to them.

With both sides' objectives clearly outlined, you now need to determine *when* is going to be the most favourable time to negotiate. Sometimes it pays to wait. Try, for example, to avoid going to ask a customer for a price rise just when your next delivery is about to run late!

Readers who recall the miners' strike of 1984 in the UK may remember how important a role the timing of it played. The Miners' Union chose to strike early in the year, when coal stocks were high and spring was approaching. Their actions did not appear to bite until much later, when Christmas was on its way. By then, their members' individual resolve to fight had been weakened as the personal cost of the strike hit their families at a very sensitive time. The strike failed. Good timing, as with so many endeavours, is essential for success in a negotiation.

CHOICE OF STYLE: WIN-WIN or WIN-LOSE?

When the foundations for your negotiation have been researched and planned, you can move on to considering the points about style discussed in the last chapter. In other words, HOW are you going to negotiate? In determining which style will be most appropriate, there are a number of considerations to be weighed up:

The repeatability of the deal. If you are looking for a long-term relationship with your opponents, your attitude towards going for a win-lose negotiation might be rather different from when you expect never to see the other side again. But in the latter case, be careful! Winning can rebound on you when, for example, the people you defeated change jobs and suddenly re-enter your life again. (This has happened to me more than once, and it can happen to you!)

The strength of the other party, with regard to both their situation and power-base, and their personalities and style.

The strength of your party and position. Building a power-base is so important that we look at it separately in Chapter 8. No-one should negotiate from a weak power-base if they can help it. If you have to, you may be forced to mask your position by bluffing your way through a competitive win-lose deal, which might be exciting but will also be risky. (I had a colleague who used to do this, regularly. It worked well for him, initially, because gun-toting shots from the hip quickly destabilised an unsuspecting side. However, in the end, he became so well known for this tactic that people began to expect it and it then became a liability.)

The importance of the deal. How badly do you need the deal? Usually, the greater the need of one side to settle, the weaker their position will be. How much will you have to give so that you get what you want in return, and how hard are you going to have to fight for it?

The timescale. If you are well prepared and the time available for discussion can be reduced, so that the other party has to deal in a rush, you may push them into giving you a highly favourable outcome. However, if *your* case is complicated, you may need, conversely, to ensure there is more time for you to present your case adequately.

Your negotiating resources. The more skilled and experienced you and your team are, the better the outcome you will rightfully seek.

The dilemma in deciding whether you should seek a competitive win-lose outcome, or alternatively a cooperative win-win, is that the styles for the two types of negotiation are incompatible.

Win-win requires an open style and mutual trust. If you set off to conduct this kind of negotiation without having checked your opponent's case first, the open, cooperative style which you must therefore display, may be seen by the other side as a display of weakness. Your opponent may therefore be inclined to drive hard for a win-lose outcome, with you being the loser. This, of course, would be the very opposite of what you had hoped for.

Conversely, if you adopt an adversarial posture to start with, just in case the other side is going to be aggressive, you will frighten your opponent into responding in kind. A win-win opportunity will never be given a chance to arise in these circumstances.

In order to overcome this dilemma, it is essential to take the following steps in the order given:

1. Set up an atmosphere of mutual respect from the very beginning.

2. Signal clearly that you are seeking a collaborative approach.

3. Wait for a confirmatory signal as to whether or not a win-win outcome is also sought by the other side.

4. Be firm and fair. (If you are not firm, your position will be seen as weak. If you are not fair, you will lose the trust and goodwill you need for a cooperative solution.)

The signalling that you seek a mutually beneficial win-win outcome will probably already have started when the meeting is set up, or before. Reinforce this when you meet.

Sometimes, however, you won't get any choice: the style, climate, tempo, agenda and timescale may all be forced upon you by the other side. If this should happen to you, the first requirement is to recognise what is happening and what style is implied.

If the attitude is benign, and it may be, all well and good. But if the opening is hostile to your intentions, you will want to be clear that before matters proceed, specific items such as agenda and timescale must be acceptable to *both* parties. You will also want to alter to your liking other important matters such as climate and tempo, using the force of your power-base and/or personality.

Changing the timing and tempo is actually a tactic frequently used in most competitive sports. It is just as relevant to negotiation. The trick is to impose *your* choice in these matters very forcefully, in an even-handed and calm way, without ever becoming enmeshed in *their* choice.

You may, for example, decide that a certain matter is not open to negotiation. As soon as it is raised, slow the pace right down and say, quite calmly but with intensity: 'Before we can continue, we must agree . . .'

If you encounter resistance to this tactic, deal with it this way:

Give no reasons or apologies.

Acknowledge that you have understood *their* **message.**

Repeat *your* **message, without malice or rising ire.**

Don't waiver, and remain confident.

You will find stubborn but unemotional repetition in such circumstances to be a very powerful tool. It is well worth trying.

CONCESSIONS

The imaginative and skilled trading of concessions lies at the very heart of successful negotiation. Exactly how to use concessions in a negotiation is discussed in the next chapter. But first, concessions have to be planned. You must first consider all of the variables in your position that you might be prepared to exchange for the objectives you seek, then value them: In other words, estimate what they would cost *you* if conceded, and what they would be worth to *the other party*. The cost to you and the value to them will rarely be the same.

Needless to say, your job is to determine which concessions would be of maximum benefit to the other side with the least cost to you. Then you should be able to trade them, ever so 'painfully' (or so you must make the other side think) – and profitably. An example might be a concession to provide product-training, which would be most useful to the buyer and relatively inexpensive for the sales team. (Note that training personnel can make the best sales people, as they are there at the customer's express invitation!) Another instance might be a buyer who allows a supplier to make part shipments of a large order. This might cost the buyer little, but be very advantageous for the seller's cash flow.

Note that **concessions should always be traded. Concessions should** *never* **be given without receiving something in exchange.**

Next, consider all the variables in the *other side's* case, and estimate the probable *cost* to them if they concede any of these to you. This will require an in-depth study of the other side's position, such as a review of financial reports, market intelligence, press reports and any other information you can lay your hands on.

Finally, value the *benefit* of the other side's variables to you. You might be surprised to find that some of these variables are quite attractive, even though you might not have thought initially of asking for them. Take special care over this phase of the planning because it can yield rich prizes.

This exercise can be taken even further. For example, several well-known automobile manufacturers have special economic analysis departments which devote their time to making complete cost break-downs for all the components they buy from their major suppliers.

This kind of analysis has the obvious advantage of giving their buyers an insight into what may be a 'reasonable' price to pay, especially for a new item. However, the analysts go further than that. They then pay particular attention to the fixed costs of the component company, such as administration, sales, rates, etc. These fixed costs are then subtracted from the estimated total cost of a component and *this* – the remainder – is the target price that the car manufacturer sets for its buyers. The philosophy is that their suppliers should seek to recover these fixed overhead costs from *other* customers, but not from them.

Similarly, skilled sales teams will do an analysis of their customers, asking questions like these: What can they afford? How many other potential suppliers do they have? How badly do they need us? How quickly can they pay? etc. Negotiators handling any kind of deal, whether they are industrial relations officers, laywers, diplomats or whatever, will all need to analyse carefully the other side's position.

Whatever you are negotiating for, if both sides are going to move from their starting position by trading concessions, the initial offer you open with *must* be more favourable to you than where you hope to settle eventually. Otherwise you will have nothing to exchange. In other words, in setting out *your* opening gambit, you need to **include a negotiating margin and aim high.**

We shall look more closely at pitching the first bid and how to trade counter-offers in the next chapter, 'Bidding', but let us first demonstrate graphically what we are doing. First, we have to set ourselves a range of **objectives**, describing what we hope to get as an acceptable deal, as follows:

|<------OUR RANGE OF OBJECTIVES------<|

We then need to focus on what might be the very best we can achieve (the **target**) by using all the skills we can muster and developing our power-base to the maximum:

|<------OUR RANGE OF OBJECTIVES------<|

OUR TARGET

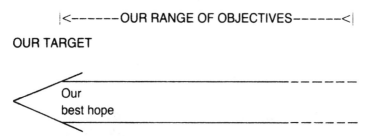

Next, identify the fallback position, beyond which we are not prepared to go *under any circumstances.*

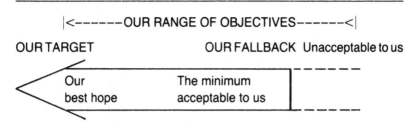

When the other side have set *their* targets and fallback positions, in the same way, there will usually be an over-lap of objectives, especially for a win-win negotiation where the style will be cooperative, rather than competitive. It looks like this:

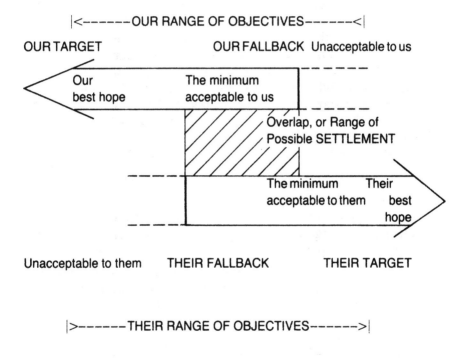

FALLBACK

Referring back to the last diagram, if the style had been a competitive win-lose, we would have been much more aggressive in setting both our objectives and our fallback position. Compare this, then, with the new situation:

63

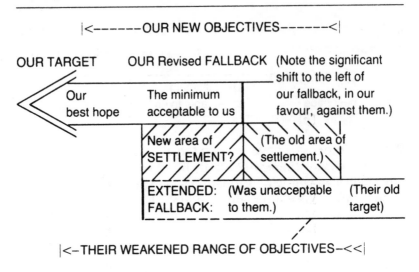

|<------OUR NEW OBJECTIVES------<|

OUR TARGET   OUR Revised FALLBACK   (Note the significant
                                     shift to the left of
Our   The minimum   our fallback, in our
best hope   acceptable to us   favour, against them.)

New area of   (The old area of
SETTLEMENT?   settlement.)

EXTENDED: (Was unacceptable   (Their old
FALLBACK: to them.)   target)

|<-THEIR WEAKENED RANGE OF OBJECTIVES-<<|

As can be seen from the above, the settlement area has moved significantly to the left in this revised diagram (i.e., in our favour). This has been achieved by setting our sights high and making our fallback position much tougher, and accordingly trapping our opponents into moving *their* fallback position towards *our* additional advantage.

Once one party's fallback position has been moved, even if just a little, settlement will nearly always finish up in the *extended* fallback zone. This is because once such a move favouring their side has started, few aggressive negotiators will want to let it go at that. They will go on pressing for the best deal they can get, and with reducing resistance there will be little to stop them.

The setting of a fallback position, sometimes known also as a 'limit', is a major part of preparation and has some strategic considerations attached. As can be seen, the setting of very ambitious limits (i.e. the *least* you can accept) will encourage competitive bargaining, which will almost certainly lead to a win-lose situation.

Nevertheless, experiments show that when both parties have consciously set their own fallback limits, concessions tend to be traded more rapidly as the parties hasten towards a mutually acceptable mid-point. Perhaps this is due to the reduction in ambiguity that arises when both parties begin to realise that

64

settlement will be possible without having to move their respective fallback positions.

THE MID-POINT

The *mid-point* is the difference between two parties' bids, and will usually indicate where settlement will finish. The above diagrams clearly demonstrate its importance.

As concessions are made by both parties, the difference between them becomes smaller and agreement becomes more likely. The area of likely settlement may not stay consistently the same, however. The final outcome will be constantly influenced by where the mid-point lies at the end of each bid.

Some negotiations will be too complex to allow a mid-point to be calculated. When this is possible, however, you will much more easily determine how to respond not only to an opening bid, but also to subsequent bids. Constant awareness of the mid-point, throughout the negotiation, is accordingly very important.

Note the following:

The higher you pitch your first bid, the more favourably positioned the mid-point will be for your side. Hence the injunction to all negotiators, 'Aim High!'

The mid-point can be moved by the positioning of each subsequent bid. Each time it is *your* turn to bid, it will be *you* who will determine the new mid-point.

You can move the mid-point in your favour by moving in smaller steps than the other side, or even by not moving at all.

This is one aspect of planning that *does* have to take place during the negotiation. We will look at it more closely in the next chapter on 'Bidding', with a worked example.

TEAM SELECTION

Suppose that you are to take part in a major negotiation of considerable complexity, involving several parties, and you have to choose your own negotiating team. The first question might be, how many people should the best-balanced team have? The easy answer is as many as you need in order to have a team qualified to cover all of the issues that are expected to be raised. However, in reality, there is another consideration which is equally important: how many people will the opposition field? Ideally, you should aim to have the same number on each side. If you field too many, you will swamp the other side. Too few, and you will be in danger of being swamped by them.

It can, on occasions, be very powerful to be a lone voice facing a large team. Clearly, one person can only have one conversation at a time. Being alone, you may therefore find it easier to control the agenda and, just as important, the pace and climate. In general, however, negotiating on your own against a larger number is *not* to be recommended. It places far too much reliance on the ability of one individual to handle all the tasks necessary – which, as we shall see, are many. In any event, a good leader should be able to control such matters as the agenda and the general negotiating environment, however big the team.

Your team selection will need to be based on the following:

Personal qualities and negotiating skills.

Functional skills and specialist areas of knowledge.

Team-playing skills.

Specific negotiating roles.

We looked at **personal skills** at the end of the last chapter. However, when planning a complex negotiation, these are not enough. You will also want to decide which specialist areas of knowledge (i.e., **functional skills**) you need to have covered.

As an example, in a commercial negotiation you may want people with specialist knowledge of:

The product or service, its application and working environment.

Specifically technical issues, such as performance, quality assurance, warranties, maintenance, later up-grading, etc.

Commercial issues, including not only price, delivery and payment terms, but any related legal issues on which you may need specialist advice in some cases (see Chapter 7). You may even wish to include a lawyer.

What is especially interesting in commercial negotiations is how rarely an experienced salesman works well as a team member, at least without specific coaching and practice. This is a warning worth heeding, because most sales negotiating teams will, quite rightly, wish to include their local sales specialist on the team to give specific advice on the customer's particular corporate personality, hidden issues, etc. Unfortunately, most sales people are rarely trained to work on a team and many find it very difficult to stand by and let others play their part. They are used to leading from the front, usually on their own.

Who makes for a good team, then? We have covered **personal skills** and **functional skills**. From the last comment above, you will note that we also need to seek certain **team playing skills**, including:

Compatibility. The team members must have respect for each other and a clear understanding of the role each member will be asked to play. You might be surprised by the opposition during the course of your negotiations, but the last thing you want is to be surprised by your own team!

Balance. This means that functional and personal skills need to be complementary across the team you choose to field. An unbalanced team is a weak team. Work by Dr Belbin at the Administrative Staff College at Henley in England has shown repeatedly that a modestly skilled management team, containing an adequate blend of the requisite skills, invariably out performs a 'team' of brilliant individuals who do not have a full blend of complementary skills, whatever the management task might be.

Credibility. This may be a self-evident requirement, but don't include colleagues who are weak in this area, unless you can shield them effectively and restrict their contributions to less sensitive issues. (I remember working for a company that received a take-over offer from a conglomerate for whom we all had the greatest respect. The offer was very well timed and we all felt positive about the deal. Then we met their chief negotiator, who was their company lawyer. He knew nothing about the product, the dynamics of the market or the real opportunities for both companies in working together. Instead, he wanted to know only about our financial controls and legal obligations to third parties. He made a good offer, but it was rejected. None of us felt the other side's representative really understood the business, or knew why a deal really made sense. He simply lacked credibility, and so – in consequence – did his company. This is still one of my greatest personal regrets.)

Personal regard by the other side. This is more than enjoying mutual respect. Research shows that when there is strong warmth of personal sentiment between the parties involved, negotiations are much more likely to be cooperative and concessions will flow more freely.

Finally, having selected a team, it is important to allocate **specific negotiating roles**, or **team duties**. These can be varied and, when necessary, carried by a team member who may also have to take on other responsibilities. The key tasks are:

Leading. Only one person can lead at any given phase of a discussion, so it is clearly essential to agree who this will be. The leader does not have to be the most senior person present, and it is not unreasonable to consider a change of leader during the course of a negotiation – for example, when stuck in deadlock. The leader *does* have to be the one who leads the discussions for your side, ensuring throughout that your plans and objectives are met. The leader may appear to be the decision-maker – but remember the power of limited authority! He or she does not necessarily have to be the *actual* decision maker.

Note taking. This person will note all agreements throughout the course of the discussions, together with specific data that you receive and other useful intelligence. Unlike a straightforward court reporter, however, the note-taker must also be prepared to take the leader to one side and offer points of information, corrections, or any other similar assistance that might be necessary to obtain a successful conclusion. This will certainly include summarising, or at least providing key points for someone else to summarise or recapitulate.

Listening. This is one of the most difficult jobs for many negotiators. Experience shows that you cannot listen and talk at the same time, so a passive (and seemingly inactive) role is essential. Nevertheless, it is a critical role. Negotiations can be won or lost by the competence and proficiency of your 'listener'. Not only must this person listen to what is said (and what is not said!), but also *how* it is said and by whom. It therefore requires the chosen individual to be an observant watcher as well.

Reviewing. Someone must also be responsible for reviewing the team's performance, internally. This might normally be done at the end of a negotiation, but reviews will also be helpful in the middle of protracted negotiations extending over several days. Don't forget that if the Leader chooses to do the reviewing, the effective team will also want to review the performance of their Leader, and so they should!

Surveillance. Some teams, through an internal hierarchical need, will include someone in authority whose role will be more than to review performance for the benefit of the team members. On such occasions, the monitoring of performance is for the benefit of the upper echelons of management not present at the negotiations. One thinks, for example, of the token KGB representative who used to accompany Russian delegations. When building *your* team, note that this can have specific consequences. Laboratory-based studies show that the presence of such a person is a major inhibitor of concession-making.

Remember, when allocating team duties, also to determine authority levels. You want to be in a position, when pushed, of saying you cannot agree to demands beyond a certain level, because they are beyond your authorised limits. This is an important tactic for limiting the size or scope of what the other side believe they might reasonably seek from you.

OPENING

To complete our careful plan there is one element left to consider: the introduction or opening of the negotiating session. The grand strategic plan for your negotiation, as we have said, should not be undertaken just as you sit down in front of the other side. However, it is clear that the planning of the later stages will require some built-in flexibility regarding details, especially if the other side is particularly mercurial or if the topic is detailed and complex. Nevertheless, the opening stages of the negotiation, and how you will handle yourself and your team, *can* be planned in detail.

This preparation should include (1) a rehearsal of what you are going to say in your opening statements and how you are going to say it, and (2) an analysis of the probable and possible opening comments which might be expected from the other side.

Some people like to plan where everyone should sit. There might be a tactical purpose in this, especially if you (or the other side) are the sort who like to play 'games', e.g., by seating the opposition in chairs which are lower, face the sun, or are otherwise uncomfortable. Personally, I find this a strange tactic to adopt. In my experience, the most favourable decisions are usually made when both sides are comfortable and relaxed. A more useful consideration should therefore be: where should each side be placed, *relative to the other*, to achieve this?

Seating people full-square opposite each other is generally considered to enhance the risk of confrontation. Avoid it if you can. Even if you plan a stormy, competitive session, such a seating arrangement will tend to raise the temperature of the discussion (or debate) even higher, making it more likely that both parties might go out of control.

Rather than seat someone opposite you, therefore, consider other options. Taking as an example the simplest possibility, a one-on-one negotiation, there are two other choices.

The most cooperative arrangement is to sit side by side (as long as you don't invade each other's personal sense of private space by sitting too close, which can be threatening and uncomfortable). Note, by the way, a subtle and additional benefit of this. If a third party should subsequently join you, your own position is then made more powerful (*unless* the third person is a colleague of the other side with much higher status. In that case, you may need to watch very carefully where the third party sits. You do not want to risk excluding the senior person and causing offence. Nor do you want that person to think you are colluding against his or her better interests.)

The most flexible seating plan is to sit 'round the corner' from the other party. This is friendly, relaxed and non-invasive. It is therefore good for encouraging a cooperative atmosphere. However, if the climate should turn aggressive, you can then distance yourself without prejudicing your position.

While on the subject of seating, in an office or a restaurant for example, note that it is usually considered best to keep your back to the wall, away from the door. You then have the other side's undivided attention. Psychologically, you also have control, especially if others should enter the room. To get the best out of the situation, you will also want to have both parties as relaxed as possible. Cue low lights and soft music? Why not, at least metaphorically!

The major benefit of planning the opening stages in so much detail is not only that you set off down the track *you* have chosen. You will also start with much more confidence. One of the best ways to check that your planning is complete is to set up a role-playing exercise. This has the merit of exposing any weaknesses in your own position. It also forces a much more rigorous analysis of how the other side will see things. (If you need additional persuasion on this point, reflect on what many musicians who perform in public are told: 'An amateur should practise, to get it right. A professional should also practise, to ensure that it doesn't go wrong.') A section on role playing is included at the end of the final chapter.

There is also something else you can do to boost confidence. As with preparing to give a public speech, planning and rehearsing the opening moments of a negotiation in your own mind, ahead of the event, can give additional personal confidence and a significant psychological boost. Interestingly, top international athletes also think themselves through the start of an important race, match or fight as part of 'psyching' themselves up. They imagine themselves in the detail of the situation that they are going to find themselves in, even to the extent of how to get to the venue, how they will feel and what they will do. They also look ahead in their minds for all the problems that they might expect to encounter, and plan how they will overcome them successfully and confidently.

On a personal level I have found this technique very helpful in many situations, including negotiating. I recommend it.

The approach you take to the opening of a negotiation can set the whole future direction of the discussions you have. Remember, **you should seek to convey an attitude that is firm, but fair.** This is best established from the very beginning. You only get one chance to make a good first impression.

Enter with an open, up-right stance, business-like but friendly if possible. You should certainly not appear aggressive, save in very exceptional circumstances. Establish early eye-contact with each member of the other side in turn, shaking hands firmly. Relax, and unless it is inappropriate, smile. If you are a student of body language, you will know that open-handed gestures are conciliatory, inviting trust.

Many people feel uncomfortable without a brief exchange of pleasantries, and your planning should take account of this. Too early an effort to get into the meat of a discussion will appear rude to such people and give the impression that you want to rush things. This might be fine for a win-lose approach, but certainly not for a win-win strategy.

When you do get down to business, your opening statements need to be positive and crisp. You will want to confirm who you are (if necessary), why you are there, what is to be achieved and how much time you feel will be needed (or is available). You need to obtain acknowledgement or agreement on all of these points, and then agree an agenda, before you proceed – listening carefully for their signals as they, hopefully, have done for yours.

For a win-win negotiation, you will want to establish a coopera-tive atmosphere from the first moment. Having checked the other party's mood and inclinations, look for an early opportunity to produce results together. If the first topic is intrinsically more difficult than some of the others, and you get agreement, the rest will be down-hill motoring. However, if you fear that this more difficult topic could become a stumbling block, or is generally rather controversial, it will help to build up some momentum by clearing more easily agreed matters out of the way first.

Even when planning a win-lose gambit, a cooperative atmosphere (being Adult-Adult rather than Parent-Child in style) is still in your favour. Unreasonable demands, even when made from a strong power-base, are still unreasonable. In such circumstances, your quarry will see you as arrogant and overbearing and may not give you the time of day. Nevertheless, without being unreasonable, you will still wish to be ambitious in making your demands. You will also be much more keen to take control of the meeting by setting the pace and the agenda. Emphasis on agreement will then become less important, and the statement of your view of things rather more so.

We have emphasised that in any negotiation, starting well is especially important. Don't leave it to chance, therefore. Plan ahead carefully. To help you do this, a check sheet for preparation is available at the back of this book. You will find it very helpful in ensuring that all the key points we have discussed have been properly covered.

Summary

- Preparation is a vital part of negotiating.

- Check out all your assumptions, as best you can.

- Identify the decision-maker on the other side.

- Formalise, value and prioritise both *your* objectives and *theirs*.

- Identify the concessions you might offer which offer the maximum benefit to the other side with the least cost to you.

- Remember, concessions should always be traded, not donated.

- Recognise that a win-win outcome can never be assumed until the other side also signals its compliance.

- A competitive opening stance by either side may turn a win-win negotiation into a win-lose one.

- Be firm but fair. Do not make 'unreasonable' demands.

- Aim high with your aspirations and first offer, to leave room for bargaining.

- Decide on your fallback position, beyond which you will not settle under any circumstances.

- Calculate and track carefully the mid-point between both sides after each bid.

- Select your team carefully, allocate the key tasks and specify authority levels.

- Plan the opening moments in your mind's eye, to build up confidence and a relaxed approach.

Useful Exercises

- From now on, whether in practice role-plays or for real, use the preparation check-sheet.

- Practise relaxation exercises, particularly in stressful situations. The secret is deep breathing, a positive mental attitude and an adult approach. When inflammatory statements are made, don't over-react. Pause and reflect. Rather than disagree outright, consider asking for a justification, or even ignoring them altogether.

- Check your own body language. When you have read Chapter 6 ('Recognising and Returning Signals'), make a point of studying the first exercise there. What signals are you giving people when you meet them? Practice giving the signals that you want to give to establish the climate you seek.

- Pick a negotiating team that you are sometimes part of. How could you and your colleagues* work better together? What lessons could you *all* learn? If necessary, buy them a copy of this book. (Don't worry, the benefits you will get will more than pay for it.)

    * [Message to these colleagues: Thank you for taking the trouble to listen, read and approve. It *was* worth it, wasn't it?]

5

BIDDING FOR THE BEST BARGAIN

'Oh Sir, we quarrel by the book, as you have books for good
manners.' *Touchstone, in William Shakespeare's As You Like It*

In order to win the most favourable deal possible, it would clearly
be best never to have to offer *any* concessions: the perfect win-
lose outcome – at least from the winner's point of view. If you
have a crushingly powerful position and will consider nothing
less than total victory, this may be a perfectly realistic strategy.
However, this situation doesn't arise very often, and in any event
can hardly be considered a 'negotiation'. As described in
Chapter 3, it is really a battle.

In a true negotiation, in order to conclude a deal successfully, both
parties will have to give some ground by exchanging concessions.
Any interested observer of negotiations may well feel that this is the
core skill required for a successful negotiation, in the true sense of the
word. Indeed it is, but let's put it into context first.

Concession-trading and bidding skills must be closely allied to
the equally important considerations of style and planning,
discussed in the preceding chapters, in order to get the best
outcome. For example, as we saw in Chapter 4, skill in trading
concessions is very much related to careful preparation. At least
six distinct kinds of planning are necessary:

1) Establishing your over-all game plan. (What style are you
going to adopt? Will you do better with a cooperative win-win
strategy, or a competitive win-lose one?)

2) Estimating what your oppponent will want, how much, and how badly.

3) Determining your objectives and fallback position.

4) Valuing and ranking the objectives that you have set yourself.

5) Weighing the value of the benefits arising from the achievement of your objectives against the cost of the concessions you may have to offer in return.

6) Comparing the costs of any concessions you may be prepared to give with the value you estimate them to have to the other side. Naturally, you will want to offer concessions with the least cost to you and the greatest value to them.

So much for the preparatory phases. Once the introductions are over, what do you do then?

Before you do anything, you have some exploring to do.

EXPLORING

The more exploring of the other side's position you can do, the stronger you will be.

You need factual information to build a successful case, and exploring early reduces later surprises. The more exploring *you* can do, the less the other side will be able to explore *your* case, and the more you will be able to control the course of the discussion. If you are to be successful, you must try very hard to reveal as little as possible about the facts relating to your position, and to concentrate on your feelings (whether true, or stage-managed in order to build up a perceived power base).

What do you need to explore?
In the list of planning phases above, and described in more detail in the last chapter, are many assumptions you had to make. *These assumptions must all be tested* by asking probing questions. You need definite answers to three main questions:

1) Does the party opposing you have the authority to conclude a

The more exploring you can do, the stronger you will be.

deal? (And if so, which person in particular?) If not, can the person who does have the necessary power join you?

2) Were you right to assume that your best strategy was to go for a win-win or a win-lose? (It isn't too late to change at this stage by

any means.) If your strategic choice was right and you were aiming for a win-lose outcome, you should continue to reveal very little of your real position at this stage, in the hope of moving the mid-point further in your favour. If, however, you feel that a win-win solution is the most appropriate, you should be exploring the possibilities and areas for a mutually beneficial settlement.

3) How accurate were you about your assessment of what the other side wants, and how strongly each element is desired? In the course of your exploring, you *must* obtain from them the full 'shopping list' of items they want to negotiate about.

If you don't do this, you fall into the infamous trap of 'salami slicing', which is a ploy *you* may want to use, but one you certainly don't want to have used against you. In brief, salami slicing involves squeezing the greatest number of concessions from the other side by making them feel each time that they can then expect to conclude a deal. You then make *further* demands upon them by bringing out additional factors. These now require even more concessions from the other side that were probably not planned, before a deal can be struck. You have thus 'sliced' off a better deal for yourself.

For an example of how this ploy works, suppose that you ask the price for a truck, and negotiate a better price. You then ask for an additional discount for buying two. When you have got that, you mention that actually you need five trucks, but of course, not at *that* price! You might then demand extra credit, free delivery and perhaps an extended guarantee.

Now suppose that you are the seller. You give the price for a truck. Having got acceptance, you advise the buyer that delivery, the tax and the licence are of course all extra. You then mention that this vehicle also comes with a variety of extras, such as spot lights, mud flaps, a radio and cruise control – which of course all have to be paid for. You then advise that it can indeed be painted in the customer's corporate colours – at a price. What about special tyres? And a service contract? Etc., etc. Oh! They wanted to take delivery to-day? That too might be extra, if you can get away with it!

In order to avoid being the victim of salami slicing, it is vital that you *establish at the outset everything that the other side wants to negotiate.* If new issues are raised later, you can then reasonably rule them out of play. Alternatively, you can start again with these new considerations on the table, but only after you have taken back all the concessions you have already offered.

Once you have established what exactly is on the other side's shopping list and how much they want each item, continue to explore across a broad front while you keep a comprehensive picture of all the issues ('the deal') in mind. Don't get side-tracked down unrewarding blind alleys. Equally important, don't get hooked into discussing the more crucial points in too much detail at the early stages. It is perfectly reasonable just to note other issues being raised, and then agree to come back to them later.

This not only helps avoid salami slicing, it also keeps discussions from foundering on what you may believe are difficult points – before their true scale of importance in the overall context is fully measured. When the whole picture is revealed, you may find that these points of 'difficulty' become relatively unimportant. You will find that these tactics are most useful in making the other party identify which of the issues are of greatest importance to them. Unimportant problems then will not be allowed to stand in the way of resolving other issues which have greater value.

If you wish to enhance the chances of a win-win outcome, exploring has another important facet. In this kind of negotiation, it is very helpful to establish areas of common ground, and search for topics on which you and the other side can agree. This is naturally far more conducive to setting a cooperative atmosphere than highlighting differences.

PROPOSING

When you have obtained your opponents' complete agenda, that is the time to start making proposals. We will look soon at factors that might affect your choice of where you pitch your first bid. But first, some general comments on making proposals. Keep these basic facts in mind:

81

Arguments cannot be negotiated; only proposals can.

Proposals advance negotiations by shedding light on the situation and indicating where the avenues to progress might be.

Proposals also help you to seize the initiative. When it is *you* who are making the proposals, it is *you* who are effectively in control. When you deny someone else's proposals, it is reasonable to make an alternative proposition: otherwise, denial becomes sterile.

Unrealistic proposals are, however, damaging. They just prolong the discussion needlessly by provoking arguments and ill-will.

Interrupting proposals provokes arguments. (So do insults!) Again, the proceedings are sidetracked and needlessly prolonged.

However, before making any proposals, remember the primary rule of negotiating: **Any concessions that you might offer must be traded for something you want.** To make proposals in this way, state your condition first, e.g., 'IF you did . . ., we could consider . . .' These conditions should be *specific* and *firm*. Because you appreciate the importance of aiming high, you will almost certainly start off by making these conditions *ambitious*, too. However, what you may be prepared to trade in exchange should preferably be vague, imprecise and general.

Thus, you might say: 'If you could reduce your price by 10%' (a specific condition), 'we could consider a means of rescheduling our delivery requirements more flexibly' (A non-specific hint of a concession).

Or, for another example: 'If you are prepared to accept the introduction of new working practices on the shop-floor' (specific), 'we will undertake to consider some form of self-funding productivity scheme' (non-specific).

SEARCHING FOR VARIABLES

When making proposals, try to be imaginative. This is where lateral thinking skills are invaluable in finding concessions that

Unrealistic proposals are damaging.

the other side will consider worthwhile, but will cost you little. This is known as *searching for variables* and is vital not only in offering concessions, but also in evaluating those you receive.

When you consider the details of both your situation and the other party's, almost everything is a potential variable. In the

83

context of selling or buying, for example, there is not just price to consider. There is also payment terms (how much, when, in what currency, by what method, with what sort of guarantee of payment, to whom, through which bank, etc.); delivery (at whose cost, to where, in what quantities, how quickly, with what sort of packaging, covered by how much insurance, with what penalties for lateness, over what sort of period, etc.); guarantees (of what specification, under what circumstances, for how long, with what penalties and bonuses, for how much, with what damages, etc.); there is consignment stock, follow-on business, licence to resell, use of trade names, free publicity of the contract and application, spare parts, addition of subsequent modifications to the product or service, buy-back, maintenance, installation, training, referrals to other parties, and almost anything else you can think of.

Alternatively, you might be in a negotiation over your pay (or someone else's). Again, there is more than just the sum of money to consider. There might be guarantees of a minimum wage, bonuses, review periods, method and frequency of payment, holidays, hours of work, overtime, insurance, pensions, health-care, concessionary prices for the company's product, the period of notice, restrictions on working for a competitor, compensation for this restriction, free meals while at work, free use of a company car, the payment of telephone rental at home, no-strike deals, flexibility of working practices or hours worked, share options, sabbaticals, office accommodation – again, a list as long as your imagination is broad.

PITCHING THE FIRST BID

We have already seen that the first bid should be as high as possible, but still realistic. Note that it is always possible for a sales team to reduce a price during a negotiation, but it is much more difficult to raise it later on. The same, in reverse, applies to buying teams. Further, experiments show that when a negotiating team expects to settle at a favourable price, they do. Conversely, **low expectations generally produce low results.** We look at this aspect of expectation and aspiration in more detail in Chapter 8, 'Improving the Outcome'.

We have also seen that the first offer is rarely the best, so it must be tested. Having introduced the concept of the *mid-point* in the last chapter, let's see a worked example of how it can be used to pitch the first (and subsequent) bids.

Suppose that you are haggling to buy an article on sale for 10 ducats. You think it reasonable that you should be able to get it for 7.50 ducats: What do you bid first?

The situation looks like this:

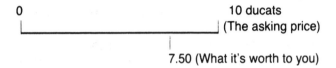

In this case, you want a reduction of 2.50 ducats, so you open with a bid the same distance further away from the other side's offer: i.e., 5 ducats.

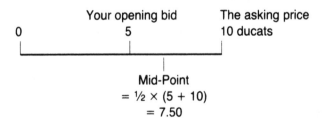

If the seller is prepared to bargain, the initial price of 10 ducats might then be reduced to 9. Accordingly, you then move towards the seller by the same amount, and offer 6. Note that the mid-point is still 7.50. If the offer is reduced to 8, you then offer 7: still a difference of one ducat. Split that between you and you have a deal at 7.50 ducats: just what you were aiming for.

85

Now you can see that by setting yourself aggressive goals and aiming high, you are in effect moving the likely settlement-point more favourably towards you. Thus, in the example above, if you had offered 4 ducats instead of 5, the mid-point would have moved from 7.50 to 7 (half of 4 + 10). Your only reason for *not* opening with this lower amount would be the risk of the seller laughing in your face and walking away. If you are going to win a better deal, that is self-evidently why your first offer should not be seen to be unreasonable.

So, the balanced decision is that you should open with the best possible offer (from your viewpoint) that you think will be acceptable, commensurate with meeting your eventual target. The same will also apply, of course, to the other party.

What would you have done if the asking price had been 15 ducats instead of 10? Clearly, if you had still opened at 5, the mid-point in this case would have moved *away* from you, from 7.50 to 10 (half of 5 + 15).

To have achieved the same end result in this case, you would have had to move in *smaller steps* than the other party, starting at the lowest offer you felt you could make. Thus, the bidding might have gone as follows:

YOUR BID	THEIR BID
'How much?'	'15 ducats!'
'I'll offer you 5' (mid-point is 15+5 divided by 2=10)	'14 as a special offer.' (i.e., down 1 ducat)
'5½' (You have raised by only ½ a ducat and the mid-point is moved to 9¾'	'13 to settle the deal, then?'
'6' (mid-point is 9½)	'10 ducats as a special favour to you?'
'6½' (mid-point is 8¼)	'9, and I couldn't do it for less.'
'7' (mid-point is 8)	'8. Let's split the difference.'
'7¼ and no more.'	

(NB: You are now close to your target, but your step towards it has been halved.)

'7¾, and don't dare tell anyone else.'

Now you decide whether you will ask for 7½, or let the other party offer it.

OFFERING CONCESSIONS

We have noted several times that when you have a concession to give, it must be traded for something from the other party that you want and value. It is also important, when you make your initial concessions, that you make them _small_ and _tentative._ If your initial offer is too large, three problems arise:

✗ **First, you give the impression that you have more to give than may really be the case.** Imagine that you are faced with demands for a 10 per cent pay rise from your work-force, but you have in fact only budgeted for 5 per cent. If your first offer is as low as 2½ per cent, your workers' negotiators might well believe, quite reasonably, that you will be prepared to concede more, but not a lot. Somewhere around 5 per cent might then appear to be quite a realistic target for both parties to settle at.

However, if your first offer is 5 per cent, the signal to the troops is that a settlement of around 7½ per cent (the revised mid-point) may be quite realistic. It is then, when revised claims above 5 per cent have to be resisted, that industrial relations turn sour: all because the wrong impression was given by the first counter-offer.

✗ **Second, you leave yourself less room for further trading.** In the example of the demand for a 10 per cent pay rise above, consider what happens if the work-force offer a _new_ concession, in return for a better pay award. If 5 per cent was really your planned 'best offer', either you will have to go beyond your original fallback and over-run the budget, or forego the concession you have been offered, or risk deadlock and the possibility of a lose-lose result. However, the employer who offers only 2½ per cent leaves room

87

to win further concessions from the other side, perhaps, and still be inside the original fallback position.

Third, by making too large an initial offer, you increase the risk of having to make a subsequent offer which is also too large. Take the wage claim example again. If you offered 2½ per cent initially, the offer by you of another 1 to 1½ per cent later on may well appear to be a valuable and hard-won advantage, worth having. However, if you offered 5 per cent to start off with, the other side might well feel that anything less than an increase of several per cent is demeaning, and hardly worth trading for concessions that they may have up their sleeve.

So, from whatever angle you look, it is important to make your offers in small steps.

Another rule relating to the offering of concessions is a little more difficult to adopt, although just as easy to understand. It is that **the weakest party usually concedes first.**

Clearly, the person making the first concession risks getting nothing in return unless the conditions attached are forcefully stated and enforced. In addition, that party also runs the risk that the first movement in position by the other side will be relatively smaller, thus moving the mid-point in their favour.

The problem is how to avoid giving the first concession without immediately becoming deadlocked, in a case where the other party is just as skilled as you. The best solution is in fact to *risk being deadlocked*. In Chapter 3, where the subject was first raised, it became apparent that deadlock is quite often the initial outcome when two experienced negotiators meet; so if it happens, consider yourself flattered! The situation will be equally uncomfortable for both parties, so you are not necessarily disadvantaged relative to the other side. It is a position that affects you both. It is only by *staying* in deadlock that the outcome is eventually prejudiced.

When you feel that *you* really must break the deadlock, the alternatives are:

Consider making a small concession, but tie it absolutely and resolutely to a condition that will give you something in

exchange. Emphasise that failure to agree may result in a lose-lose outcome. Few experienced negotiators, genuinely wanting to deal, will allow *that* to happen.

Try diversionary tactics: offer something which is of little or no value to you, or agree to trade minor concessions simultaneously (i.e., both parties move at the same time).

Set a deadline. Because so many negotiators try not to give the first concession, it most often happens that concessions only start to flow as the deadline approaches: which is why setting deadlines can be so very helpful. Most significant concessions are traded at the end of a negotiation. To help counteract being too generous when time starts to run out, it is helpful to have a personal rule: *don't make large concessions near a deadline.*

(Better still, never make large concessions at all!)

Sometimes, you may be asked to give a concession that you had not planned, in exchange for something you value. It is then very important to:

State that this is a one-off occurrence due to exceptional circumstances, which could not be repeated. (Otherwise, it might become a standard part of future packages.)

Try always to couple the concession you offer with another concession of similar magnitude in return, so that your case is not weakened.

Sometimes, you may be asked for concessions that you feel should not be given under *any* circumstances. This is no problem: it is why you set yourself some fallback parameters in your planning, so do not feel uncomfortable about refusing. Your tactics should be to:

Build up the concession's cost to you in the mind of the other side, explaining why it is a completely unrealistic request.

Minimise the importance to them of the concession requested.

Consider offering alternatives that are more acceptable to you.

RECEIVING CONCESSIONS

Concessions should not only be given reluctantly, they should also be received reluctantly. This rule may seem a paradox, but the reason is simple. If you accept an offer too quickly, you leave the thought with the other party that they have given you too much (which may result in their withdrawing the offer later, if they can). You thus leave them feeling that they have probably got a bad deal, and you will almost certainly prejudice your chances of winning further concessions. This is not the best situation to be responsible for. And don't forget, you may also have to meet them again on some other occasion!

Therefore, accept concessions slowly, with apparent pain. This is known as flinching and is practised by most skilled negotiators: 'That's a very disappointing offer.' 'I don't know that I could persuade my colleagues to accept . . .' 'Is that the best you can do?' 'That's nothing like good enough.' However reasonable the offer, there may always be more to come – *if* you don't seem too enthusiastic about what you've gained so far.

Alternatively, you might choose to give no reaction at all to an offer. This strategy is especially difficult to deal with, as we saw in Chapter 3. The other party, enthusiastic to deal, may well then be driven to make yet further concessions in order to please you. The less pleasure you show, the more they must go on to offer you.

LINKING CONCESSIONS

You have now capitalised on many of the skills you need. You have sought out the concessions you want, assertively and confidently, and won them in return for items of value to the other side which are of minimal cost to you. You have shown suitable pain at the woeful inadequacy of the 'generous' offers made to you, and have accepted them slowly and reluctantly.

There is, however, another important consideration, and it relates to the principle of keeping all of the issues in mind as the negotiation proceeds. If you start to negotiate detailed points item by item, the danger is that you will get picked off, item by item, giving the advantage on each occasion to the other side. Before you know it, the total package will be very unattractive to you, although you will be committed to it. The secret, therefore, is to *link all the issues into one package.* A net loss on the concession-trading regarding one item can then be set off against a benefit somewhere else.

The negotiation might run something like this:

'If you give us A, we could consider giving you X'.

'In return for X, *and* Y which we also need, we would be prepared to offer you A *and* B as well.'

'I don't think we would want to consider offering X *and* Y, unless you gave us A, B *and* C.'

'We could certainly look at giving you A, B and C, but then we should have to ask for X, Y *and* Z'.

And so on.

Note how each offer is attached to a linking condition. Each of the elements, A, B, C etc., will normally have differing values, but the ground is now set for an almost infinite variety of possibilities for both parties to juggle with. This is naturally much more sophisticated than playing with just one issue, with an eye to moving the mid-point in your favour. But by linking all the issues, you make your position very powerful.

Diplomats are particularly adept at linking seemingly unrelated issues together in a way which, admittedly, often baffles the public. One thinks, for example, of territorial ownership and international air-fares (Gibraltar), or 'Human Rights' and trade issues (Helsinki Accord). You might try this too.

However, it won't *always* be in your best interests to link issues: it depends on what has happened before, your style and also your power-base. Whenever you are in a negotiation, it is useful to ask yourself:

'Have the issues all been raised separately? Can I link them more profitably into one package?'

And then, conversely:

'Am I being offered an overall package? Should I break it down into component pieces and try to negotiate item by item?'

An excellent example of this sort of thinking can be found in the computer world. Imagine that a purchasing team want to buy a complete package. They will certainly want to link all the separate deals together. The sales side, however, will want to do the opposite. They will try and break their offer into a myriad of smaller, separated issues such as:

hardware	documentation
software	project management
training	installation
support	terminals
maintenance	communications

The computer salesman might only see this as an effort to sell as many of his or her company's products as possible, but the sales manager is also thinking of squeezing out the best deal possible. The buying team might try to negotiate item by item, but this is hard work and can be defended against by a strict price list. The purchasers' best strategy, nevertheless, is *not* to play it the seller's way if at all possible. All the items should be wrapped into one project, where individual components are not separately priced as such, and negotiated from there.

Conversely, if you are first of all offered a package deal, then it is good tactics to break it down into smaller components, so you can get the seller to justify each item. This will allow you to chip away, piece by piece, at the seller's initial offer.

An example of this might be a multi-site company which has, in the past, traditionally negotiated Group-wide contracts of supply. Having done this successfully and reduced the price levels once, it is a very attractive option subsequently to break the contracts up, back to site level, to encourage local suppliers to discount even further. Several large companies are now doing this successfully.

RATES OF CONCESSION-GIVING

Quite a large amount of research has been done on what influences the rate of concession-giving in a negotiation. Note that there is an optimum frequency with which to trade concessions.

Clearly, if you are too slow, the other side will be reluctant to offer you anything for fear that you may abuse their offer. Equally, too rapid an offering of concessions can only lead the other party into feeling that if they sit still, all the concessions they want will eventually come tumbling out.

Having said that, the time taken to settle an agreement is proportional to the rate and scale of concessions offered by each party, as personal experience would suggest. Large concessions may accelerate a conclusion, but naturally, the outcome for the party giving them will be poor. Fortunately, experiments show that cooperation is a function of concession *frequency*, not size. The skilful player will therefore be happy to make regular concessions, but each one will be small. This is both more effective and more productive than offering a few large concessions.

It is interesting to recall the comments earlier on about setting fallback or 'limit' positions: they tend to accelerate the concession rate. Note, however, that aggressive fallback positions, resulting from high aspirations, are more likely to lead to competitive bargaining and win-lose outcomes.

PAUSING FOR BREATH

When negotiations are complex, it can be very difficult to be sure that you are not going to be led down a blind alley or trapped into a less favourable deal. Sometimes you will need time to think and re-plan your strategy.

It is an excellent negotiating tactic, therefore, to *summarise,* from time to time, just what you think your discussions have covered. Make sure that the other side sees things in the same light as you – it is very important to ensure that you have not misunderstood each other. Probing ambiguities before they become major misunderstandings is an important task of any negotiator who is seeking a long-term settlement.

Summarising can also give time for new ideas and re-appraisal of old ones. Sometimes, however, you will need even more time. This is where you seek a *recess*. (The very first time you ask for 'time out', you may well feel a little strange. Nevertheless, it is a perfectly reasonable request, and can be a very valuable tool. Be brave, and remember that all the best negotiators call for a recess sometimes. It is the weaker or less skilled who shy away from doing so.)

Summary

- Concessions should be valued, in the preparation phase, and then exchanged during bidding for concessions of equal or higher value to you.

- Assumptions need to be tested in the exploration phase, when you may reveal your feelings, perhaps, but not your actual position.

- Establish what is on their agenda (i.e., get their full 'shopping list') and explore across a broad front. Do not get drawn into discussing detailed points too soon.

- Keep the whole deal in mind as discussions proceed.

- Proposals help advance negotiations and assist the proposer in seizing the initiative. They need to be realistic, however, and should not be interrupted.

- Proposals which might only be general to start with should be preceded by conditions which must be specific and firm.

- Be imaginative in looking for as many variables as possible in the other side's position.

- Aim high with your proposals.

- Remember that the weaker party will usually concede first.

- Encourage the other side to give you concessions by setting deadlines.

- Your concessions should be small and tentative, but regular, in order to encourage the other side to respond.

- Accept concessions slowly, with apparent pain (i.e. 'flinch').

- If you are offered a package deal, split it up. If you are offered a range of items, search for a global package.

- Summarise regularly, and feel free to suggest a recess when you need time to plot your course further.

Useful Exercises

- Think of a simple negotiating situation that you might well face, either at work or at home. Now try to find as many variables as possible which might be linked into winning a better deal.

- Make a point during your next negotiation of seeking a recess. (Don't forget to summarise the overall position before you do this, and perhaps again when you reconvene.) How did it feel? It wasn't too bad, was it? Did you come up with any new variables or issues that you hadn't thought of before you recessed? What was the other side's reaction?

- In future win-win negotiations, consider making more frequent concessions (in exchange, of course, for reciprocal benefits), but make them smaller. This should enhance not only the quality of the outcome, but also the speed with which the talks are concluded.

- Next time you are offered a package deal, split it up. Equally, when you are offered a range of items, try to amalgamate them into one package. Did this give a better result than you had hoped for? Did you find it gave you more leverage?

6

RECOGNISING AND RETURNING SIGNALS

'I really do not see the signal.' *Southey's Life of Nelson*

Empathy and ego-drive are said to be the hallmarks of a good salesman. They are also essential characteristics for any strong negotiator. Ego-drive is necessary for the strength of purpose you will need in order to achieve your objectives. Empathy is important for gauging the effect you are having on the other side and picking up the signals they are giving you.

Some signals may be unintentional, indicated by speech, reactions, gestures and body posture. Other signals will be deliberate messages, but in code. These coded signals are a very important part of negotiating, and it is essential that you become adept at not only picking them up, but also giving them in return.

You might well wonder why these messages have to be coded or obscured, if they are so important. The reason is because a bald statement can often be too blunt a tool, which might damage your case rather than assist it. Signals are often used to hint that a concession is available or, with some modification, could be acceptable. Making the position overtly clear might make the signaller appear to be in a position of weakness.

Two examples might demonstrate this point. First, what about the flirtatious wink as a signal? If it is ignored, no real harm is done. A more overt statement of amorous intentions might well have resulted in a slap across the face!

A second example might be taken from the field of diplomatic negotiations. Why did the Chinese exchange table-tennis players and orchestras with the West? It was a signal, on a relatively minor matter, that there was a willingness to consider negotiations on bigger issues.

Alternatively, signals might be used not as an invitation to proceed but rather as a warning not to. You might, for example, signal obliquely, 'Don't press your claims too hard here, or we might have to retaliate'. If you said this openly, you might either be accused of imagining problems ahead that were not in fact there, or worse, being obstructive. Signals are therefore a very useful way of preserving a cooperative atmosphere.

An example of a signal being used effectively might be when a prospective customer rings up to say, 'We shan't be letting this contract until to-morrow. However, you have put so much trouble into preparing your bid, we thought it would only be fair to let you know that your offer wasn't competitive'.

The signal is clear: the decision won't be made until to-morrow. There was no point in telling you that, unless they thought you would or could use the information. Clearly, you are being given a second chance to bid.

However, the customer couldn't possibly have said simply, 'You are too expensive. Have another go.' First, he might then be accused of giving you an unfair advantage over the competition (which he is, but he is making sure that the formal initiative comes from you, not him). Secondly, he would be in danger of appearing too keen to buy from you. If you were given *that* signal, you would be less keen to reduce your price!

In fact, to highlight the point, the customer could have signalled even more clearly. He might have said, 'Your bid is uncompetitive *as it stands*.' The intention is clear: your bid could be changed if you want to be sure of getting the business.

Whether you take note of this signal or not depends on whether you believe the tip-off. If you choose to interpret it as 'just a negotiating position', it would clearly be impolite to say that you think the buyer is bluffing (i.e., lying!). Equally, you won't want to lose the business, so you will have to help the buyer save face. You can do this by answering with another signal. For example: 'Well, that's very helpful information. Thank you. But are you sure you have compared like with like in comparing our

bid with others? You did note that we are offering . . ., did you?'
The buyer might continue to brazen it out, but if your tone of
voice makes it clear that you don't believe that you are uncompetitive, you have also made it very clear that you are at least
offering the prospective customer a neat escape route for saving
face.

Signals also can be very useful for indicating what sort of a
negotiator you are. This is clearly important if you wish to offer
the other side a win-win deal, especially when you suspect that
they may be expecting you to go for a competitive win-lose one.

Another function of signals, whether given intentionally or
otherwise, is to suggest areas that might be particularly profitable
for the other side to explore. For example, you might be told: 'Our
main concern is product reliability.' This is a clear signal that
guarantees will probably be far more important than price – so
don't waste your time talking about your price-competitivity in
the market place. Concentrate instead on your product's performance and its ability to meet the needs of the application.

You should also use signals to highlight what your needs are,
to suggest what you might give up in exchange for having these
needs met, and indicate the degree of your commitment to a
given position. There is a world of difference between 'We would
like to have . . .' and 'We must have . . . or we can't proceed
further.' 'Would like' and 'must have' are signals of two very
different requirements.

COMMUNICATION AND BARRIERS

Most people know full well the general principles of good oral
communication: Give clear, straightforward information, unam-
biguously, in digestible bites which can be confirmed by your
listeners as having been comprehensively understood before you
move on.

Good communication skills are of course particularly vital
when negotiating, especially skill in the more subtle aspects of
giving coded messages or signals. The greatest problem in this
area appears to be recognising *barriers* to good communication

and dealing with them properly. These barriers fall into a number of categories:

Language barriers. In general, people know that if they are meeting someone from a different country, or even a different part of the same country (if there are strong regional accents or dialects), they need to speak slowly, clearly and carefully, using words which they can be sure that the other side will understand.

Putting this into practice, however, invariably seems to be forgotten as we warm to our task. This is in part because it seems to be human nature to believe that the way we speak is 'normal' and the speech of everyone who speaks differently is 'odd'. The only way to find out if *your* accent is difficult for outsiders to understand is to ask, honestly and with humility, someone from outside your locality whom you can trust. If you don't believe what you are told, you may be fooling yourself!

A problem related to difficulties with accents is the misunderstanding of local *patois* or phraseology. This is especially true of familiar expressions that do not translate word-for-word into the meaning you wish to convey. One thinks warmly of such examples as 'Why aye, man' ('yes'); 'in a jiffy' ('soon', although some might interpret this to mean 'in a padded envelope'); 'We've been clobbered by a price-hike' (an expression of mixed parentage, meaning that we have suffered a price rise – as *you* might guess, but not someone whose mother-tongue is not English); 'What time do you knock off?' (meaning 'finish work', but other interpretations may be possible!); and many other colourful but hard-to-translate expressions.

Another barrier can be unintentional ambiguity, such as talk of 'an improved price' (improved from whose point of view?) or the question 'Have you got it straight?' (Does this mean 'Have you understood me?', or is it to be taken literally?). American-British misunderstandings arising from incorrect translation can be a special problem, because we *think* we speak the same tongue. I remember asking a potential American supplier for a copy of their latest 'accounts'. As an Englishman, I was asking for their financial report. As Americans, they thought I was after a list of all their customers.

Translation problems can occur even inside a national border.

During the introduction of unmanned automatic railway crossings in the UK in 1965, flashing red road-traffic lights were installed, accompanied by a sign that read 'Stop here while lights flash'. This sign was not a totally helpful injunction in some regions of the country. Two years later, the signs had to be amended to read 'Stop here *when* lights flash'. What, you might wonder, was the problem? In many parts of Yorkshire and Lincolnshire, 'while' does not mean 'when', but 'until'.

Ambiguity can also arise through a lack of imagination of what other interpretations might be possible (I rather like the example of the story that starts, 'Two girls went for a tramp in the woods') or a lack of thought about what the other side really needs to know. Questions asked may be answered, but the questions that *should* have been asked, if the questioner had known better, go unanswered. An everyday example of this is the giving of directions to visitors to a town. All too often, people are delighted to offer assistance, but they often forget to mention things that will confuse the new-comer (e.g., that major road off to the left which *they* know should be ignored, but you don't because they forgot to tell you), or they forget about things that have changed recently (the shop on the corner has changed its name, the road you are told to take is now a one-way street in the wrong direction, etc.). Communication failures like this can arise in negotiating, too.

Just occasionally, ambiguity may suit your purposes – as in the school report for the boy who had done no work and yet came top of his class in the end-of-term exams. His teacher was sure that the boy had been cheating, but couldn't prove it. He wrote in the boy's school-report, rather adroitly, 'Johnny continues to forge his way ahead.' Usually, however, ambiguity should be assiduously sought out and removed.

Other difficulties arise, especially in the presence of foreigners, for those who use long, rambling sentences, such as: 'At this moment in time, all things being equal and fully considered, we believe that in the light of present circumstances it wouldn't be unreasonable to seek a marginal improvement in our return with regards to your specific off-take of XYZ.' A straightforward 'We have looked at the situation carefully and regret we need to raise our prices for XYZ' would be much better. Double negatives should also be assiduously avoided. They might not only be confusing in themselves, they can also be misinterpeted. In some languages a double negative is used to *reinforce* a negative statement.

Equally irritating is the use of specialist jargon and technical language, which cannot reasonably be expected to be within the grasp of your audience. The computer industry has provided wonderful examples of this, although it appears that at long last they may have begun to mend their ways. Your company's specialists and technologists need watching carefully when they attempt to communicate with lay people, for experience shows that few people are willing to acknowledge that they do not understand specialists' terms.

Finally, there is the use of words in the wrong context, mainly through ignorance. There is a world of difference, for example, between 'infer' (determine from what *someone else* says) and 'imply' (suggest something indirectly in what *you* say). You might be very keen to get a 'disinterested' arbiter involved in a dispute, but one hopes not an 'uninterested' one. You might well be happy to report that you 'expected' the next price-rise, when it comes, but you would have been wiser if you had 'anticipated' it. Sometimes it is only pedantic to complain about misuse of words, but on other occasions the whole meaning of a phrase can be inverted or made subject to misinterpretation – and a serious misunderstanding can result.

Communication barriers arising from language problems are largely due to a lack of imagination and empathy towards the other party. If you are having difficulty in communicating something, you should be able to pick this up from the signals you receive from the other side (whether verbal or otherwise) *before* the difficulty becomes a major problem.

Psychological or attitudinal barriers. These come in various guises and, again, require some empathy or sensitivity to overcome. While you are presenting your case, you might pick up a strong sense of disagreement, for example. It is important to be alert to these sorts of feelings. If you suspect a strong emotional antagonism from the other side, the chances are that they *already* have a fixed idea of what you are going to say next, and will not be listening fully to what you actually say.

Thus, people who expect you to have a strong message, whether they are in disagreement with or in support of your case, will also have a fixed idea of what you are *probably* saying that may keep them from registering what you *are* saying. The skilful negotiator needs to be fully alert to this. (The motorist who ran out of petrol in the story related in Chapter 3, for instance, would perhaps have been better off if he had learned this lesson.)

Sometimes barriers are erected by using emotive language at too early a stage in a negotiation, or because of perceived social (or intellectual) inferiority or superiority. If one side is excessively aggressive or shy, relative to the other side, that too can present a fertile breeding ground for mistrust and misunderstanding; so also can any other mismatch of personality, or even status. These are therefore important considerations when planning the composition of one's negotiating team (see Chapter 4).

Physical barriers. Such impediments tend to be external to the parties involved, and so can generally be more easily overcome than the others we have been discussing. The problem might be an uncomfortable chair, lack of space, noise, room temperature or even a personal disability such as deafness. Because close concentration (by both parties) is so important, you should have no qualms about being politely assertive in dealing with such problems.

Some physical barriers can be more difficult to remove, such as a shortage of time, or geographic separation which makes meeting difficult. (Note: negotiation by telephone is categorically *not* recommended.) If either of these barriers should interfere with good communications, you should work hard to find ways of removing it, or if you cannot, at least recognise that your negotiation will be much more difficult.

LUBRICATING COMMUNICATIONS

So much for the negative side of communications. Removing barriers to mutual understanding is a major requirement in any negotiation, but you can do better than that. *The positive and imaginative use of language* can improve your case further than you might appreciate.

The case was put very forcibly as long ago as the turn of the century in a book by a certain Ernest Pertwee, *The Art of Effective Speaking*:

> Words are instrumental of music; an ignorant man uses them for jargon; but when a master touches them they have an unexpected life and soul.
> Words may be said to be as silver. The creation of vivid ideas, gold.

Whilst simplicity of speech is generally very important, you can enhance your case on occasions by the appropriate use of golden metaphor, simile and hyperbole. Perhaps you may have heard some of these examples before:

'Persuading your Accounts Department to pay on time is like pushing water up-hill.'

'Your delivery schedules are as slow as molasses in January.'

'If my boss gets to know of this crazy deal I'm offering you, he'll tell me that the profit we'll be making won't cover the postage stamps for my letter of dismissal.'

'Your shipping department doesn't seem to know whether it's Good Friday or Sheffield Wednesday.'

Very scathing comments can be quite acceptably packaged in good humour, and made to weigh heavily for you. Alternatively, you can forsake purple prose and adopt a 'bluer' tinge, the politest form of which might be 'Cobblers!'

An expression like this is a most powerful statement. It suggests total opposition to an unreasonable deal, without giving the other side *any* formal argument against which it can debate. It is 'unarguable' and works especially well with people whom you know well enough not to offend. (Shop-floor staff seem to delight in 'Cobblers!' in particular, and for its power, so do I!)

INADVERTENT SIGNALS

Some signals occur as much by accident as by design. Sending such messages inadvertently needs to be very carefully guarded against. A simple request for a price 'right away, because we have just run out' is a wonderful signal to receive. It says that your customer has a problem and won't mind paying a little more. Likewise, accepting a tentative proposal too quickly is a damaging signal to give. It says that you consider the offer to be very generous. Making a concession that is large, in the context of the negotiation, also says that you have even more to offer (whether you really have or not).

There are those who have made a scientific study of a particular form of inadvertent signals: body language. This may perhaps be a subject that some will treat with scepticism. However, personal experience may suggest to you that its study has some merit. For example, perhaps you have found that those who cover their mouth and face when speaking may well be telling lies, or are perhaps at least uncertain about the truth, as studies of body-language suggest. Certainly, if the other side leans forward towards you, that is a strong signal that you have their attention, and probably their agreement. It is also said that if people cross their arms, legs or ankles, they are being defensive; they may either be lying, or they disbelieve *you*. However, it could also be in some cases a habitual pose with little useful significance to a negotiator.

Experienced observers of body language look for signals from both the individual parts of the body (fingers, hands, arms, shoulders, legs, feet and eyes) and the whole ensemble. It is claimed that these signals can indicate defensiveness, doubt or a judgemental attitude. They might also show hostility, aggression, cooperation, decision-making, agreement or even physical attraction.

Perhaps the most useful aspect of body language is *mirror-imaging*, or subconscious mimicry. If one side mirrors the other's posture, that is an excellent sign of potential accord. This can be a most powerful way to put others at their ease and it is a technique widely used by those involved in counselling. To adopt the same pose as the person opposite you is a very useful way to demonstrate a sense of agreement and generate a relaxed atmosphere. (You can of course do the opposite, if you should wish.)

It is claimed that studying body language can also help you to identify the leader of a group, if it is not otherwise apparent.

According to practitioners, the real leader will almost certainly be the person who initiates a stance (such as folded arms, elbows on the table, or whatever) which is then copied by the rest of the group.

For an excellent review of this subject, I can warmly recommend a book by Allan Pease, entitled *Body Language*, which you will find interesting in regard to both the workplace and general social interaction.

There have been several recent advances in the study of body language which may give extra insight into understanding inadvertent signals. Interestingly, many show the importance of watching people's eyes.

For example, researchers at Washington University in St Louis, Missouri, have studied blinking. They believe that blink rate and duration are not at all random and haphazard. Rather, they have found them to indicate feelings such as anxiety, boredom or fatigue. While this particular information may be of most relevance to tiring car drivers, for example, (and the US Air Force, which has tested a technique based on this research to monitor the vigilance of its pilots) perhaps more interesting to a negotiator will be the finding that blinking can also indicate when we make decisions or store information. Using electrodes and video recordings, the researchers showed that *when we blink, information temporarily ceases to be taken in and processed.* You might find, one day, that this is quite an important piece of knowledge to you.

Two special techniques resulting from research in this area are also worth mentioning because of their special interest to the negotiator. The first is called the 'Facial Action Coding System' and comes from the Human Interaction Laboratory in San Francisco. Reportedly, it claims to be able to distinguish between genuine and false smiles. Apparently, for a genuine smile, the cheeks and corners of the lips move up, the muscles around the eyes tighten to make 'crow's feet', and the skin around the eyebrow is pulled towards the eye. Now, all broad smiles can apparently push the cheeks up and produce crow's feet, but only the genuine article produces a noticeable lowering of the skin below the eyebrow to give a skin droop. All other smiles are said to be false.

The second technique, also from the States, is called 'Neuro-Linguistic Programming', or NLP for short. The claim is that trained practitioners can 'mostly get pretty well anyone they talk with to do what they want done.' No doubt we shall be hearing a lot more about this technique if the claim is valid.

The starting point for the NLP claim is the premise that when people make decisions, they habitually use their senses of sight, hearing and feeling, usually unconsciously, in a particular and strategic fashion. Once a trained observer has established which strategies a person is using, that information can be used to influence what the person decides. Right-handed people are said to work in a different mode from those who are left-handed, but in general, it is postulated that by watching someone's reactions to what is being said, a number of internal review mechanisms can be identified and tracked. The main thing to watch is the listener's eyes.

First, the listener will picture in his 'mind's eye' what is being said. The right-handed person is said to tense his or her shoulders, look upwards and breathe shallowly, high in the chest, while reviewing what has been said. When looking to the left, the person is probably remembering an image of something that happened before. When looking to the right, he or she is probably constructing a *new* mental picture in response to the message being given.

In the next stage, the listener's shoulders will be set back a bit and if breathing is more even, from the middle of the stomach, with a level gaze, the observer's attention is switched from mental pictures to sounds: A look directed horizontally to the left, it is said, indicates that the listener is recalling sounds heard in the past, but a look to the right indicates that new ideas are being put mentally into words.

The third phase consists of a look downwards, with a hand placed near the chin or mouth. Most probably, the listener is having a mental 'talk' with himself. The fourth stage, indicated by relaxed shoulders and breathing low in the stomach, signals that gut feelings are being reviewed to help the listener decide what may be acceptable, and what may not be, in what the speaker has said.

According to NLP theory, if the listener's response is anything other than positive, it is our fault (the speaker's) for failing to make use of the information made available to us by the listener as we were presenting our case. The key to success appears to lie in making the listener 'comfortable' when you seek a favourable view, in part by watching the person's reactions carefully. For example, you may have presented wordy, rational arguments when the listener was trying to form visual images of your ideas. It would have been better to offer less logic and more imagery in what you said at this stage. Similarly, when the listener is in the 'hearing' mode, it is no good asking for his or her feelings. It would be better to ask how the proposals 'sounded'. If you want to know how the listener 'feels' about a proposition, it is better to wait until the final stage.

The NLP technique is said by practitioners to be very useful. Its accuracy may well depend upon the cultural background of your listener, but it is interesting to note that research is being conducted into such areas of human response, and we may be unwise to ignore it.

In order to conceal his actual emotions and feelings, whatever the analytical techniques that may be employed by the other side, the experienced negotiator will certainly work very hard at trying NOT to react to what is being said (the poker-face approach). This has much merit – although no doubt such 'poker players' are not averse to trying the occasional bluff, for instance a contrived false signal such as a shake of the head and a sharp intake of breath when listening to a proposal being made.

Thus, oral signals may, in the last analysis, be the best. They tend to be deliberate and are usually unambiguous, if you know the signaller's 'code'.

INTERPRETING SIGNALS

Establishing the hidden meaning behind most oral signals is not that difficult, once your mind is open to all the possibilities. Consider some of the following:

Buyer:

'We would like you to come to discuss your quotation at 10.30 a.m. We will book lunch for you in our staff canteen.'

Clearly this is an indication that your bid was of more than passing interest; it must have been to merit that amount of time.

Salesman:
> 'How do you feel about our suggestions on payment terms, made in our offer to you?'

This suggests that if you don't like them, they could probably be improved!

Trade Union Official:
> 'Our people think that they should be paid more for greater flexibility.'

But this clearly concedes that they do have to be more flexible. Note also the phrasing: 'Our people think . . .' This is quite different from 'We insist.'

Manager:
> 'We are going to have to consider making some redundancies.'

Obviously, however, he or she is open to offer, as to where they should come from, and when, for example.

Signals can also indicate negotiating style. For example, 'We must have a price reduction *now* of x per cent or we will go elsewhere' is specific and final. It is clearly distributive (win-lose) in tone. Compare it with 'We would like to cut our overall costs by about x per cent this year.' This is neither final nor specific, but rather a tentative suggestion indicating an integrative (win-win) approach.

Other indications of true intent include phrases such as the following ('translations' in parentheses):

'As things stand . . .' ('But we are keen to deal with you in principle.')

'I don't have the authority to . . .' ('But don't give up. Why not ask my boss?')

'We don't normally . . .' ('Only when we are pushed, do we . . .')

'We would find it very difficult to . . .' ('But push harder and we might': otherwise, they would have said 'No'.)

'We liked your offer . . .' ('And we think with a bit more pressure on you, we shall probably like it even more!')

'I won't negotiate under duress.' ('I don't like your sanctions, but I will negotiate under more amenable conditions.')

'We can meet to discuss this problem, but our position is not negotiable.' ('Oh yes it is! – or what is there to discuss?')

IGNORED SIGNALS AND FEINTS

Sometimes, signals are ignored. This may be tactical, but in general signals should be rewarded with some kind of response: otherwise you increase the risk of deadlock and stalemate.

If your signals are being ignored, *don't* start giving concessions! This just reinforces the wisdom of ignoring them. Instead, re-package the signal and repeat it. If you say, for instance, 'We couldn't consider a rebate for that volume.' (Meaning 'We *could* give a rebate for a larger slice of the action'), and this is ignored, repackage the signal.

You might rephrase your first statement and say, 'The volume you are proposing to allocate is *too small* to merit a rebate', and if that is ignored, try 'We could consider a rebate *for more business*', and so on. The eventual response may be negative, but you should still insist on *getting a response* of some sort before dropping what might be a very interesting proposal that you are trying to make.

There is one occasion where you will specifically need to ignore a signal: when the signal is false, or a *feint*. However, the feint is a useful weapon to deploy yourself, on occasions.

The feint is a red herring. The technique is to concentrate very heavily on an issue about which you really care very little. Having suckered the other side into buying this performance, you then slowly and graciously concede the point, in return for the concession you did *not* signal was of interest to you, but in fact you needed badly. Done well, it works every time. If you are going to use this ploy, however, do make sure that your signals are clear. Otherwise the other side will only be confused.

110

TIPS

The best advice, on signalling in general, is to *listen to the 'music' behind the words*. People do *not* always mean what they say. (Sometimes they tell you tall stories.) Neither do they always *say*

Listen to the music behind the words.

what they mean! But they will usually indicate or hint at their real intentions. The job of the skilled negotiator is to pick these signals up, and use them intelligently.

Signals do not make settlement inevitable and they cannot, on their own, remove conflict. They can however lubricate the mechanism of settling.

Even when in a debate, if you wish to, you can signal positively that you are *not* seeking a confrontational debate even if your follow-up statement or question might then turn out to be quite aggressive. Note the positive, conciliatory tone of these examples:

'May I seek clarification of just what you mean by ...?'
'Can I ask a question ...?'
'Did I understand you correctly, that you are saying ...?'
'If I may say so ...'

These are all useful phrases that can be used to preface what might be very direct and cutting remarks. Apart from giving some warning of what is to follow, they also introduce a certain civility into the tone of the proceedings, if used cautiously. Be careful, though: a comment preceded by 'With respect' tends to grate. It has been used too often, *without* respect, to have any validity today.

We have already indicted that ignoring signals is generally not recommended. This will only prolong the argument and may aggravate it. The secret is to talk less and listen more. Not for nothing are strong negotiators often the silent types! So, when you receive a signal, *explore* it. If you are told that your offer is unacceptable 'as it stands', find out under what conditions it could be acceptable. If a supplier 'doesn't normally give extended credit', find out when he does.

Never ignore a good signal! Admiral Nelson may have done, but he wasn't noted for being an outstanding negotiator. On the contrary, he was a fighter!

Summary

- Signals are a vital part of negotiating, whether you are giving them or receiving them. They can indicate the style of negotiation, what your (and the other side's) needs are, degrees of commitment and areas for profitable exploration.

- Clear and unambiguous communication is an important part of giving signals. Communication skills require imagination and empathy.

- The many barriers to good communication should be watched for and eliminated.

- Listen carefully to the 'music behind the words'.

- Beware of giving unintentional signals, but keep a sharp lookout for those given by others.

- Signals should not be ignored, unless you know they are false. When received, they should be explored.

Useful Exercises

- This is the exercise you were referred to in Chapter 4 ('Preparation'). If you can bear it, look at yourself in a full-length mirror. Ask yourself, and others, what subtle signals are you giving when you enter a room, shake hands and sit down? Practise putting people at their ease – and establish what you might be doing, subconsciously, that puts people on their guard. Watch other people too, and learn from them. Ask colleagues to comment on your next performance at a negotiation.

- As a simple demonstration of how easy it is to misunderstand seemingly quite straightforward communications, try the following with a group of people: (It makes for a good party game, by the way).

  Give one person a simple diagram, and ask him or her to describe it to the others in words only. The others must then draw the picture that is described to them. It is best if the others are out of sight, and they must be told not to ask questions or make any other noise that might indicate confusion or doubt. You will find that only truly skilled communicators, who think ahead and imagine clearly the problems that lie in store for those who are listening to them, will be successful. (Note that any misunderstandings are usually not the fault of those who are listening, but of the person talking.) An example of the sort of diagram you might use is given below. (Start off by making it simpler if you wish, and more complicated later, perhaps.) How accurately have the others been able to reproduce it?

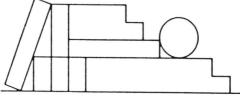

- Listen to public statements from diplomats, politicians and the opposing sides in an industrial dispute, reported in the news media. What might they really be saying? What signals are they sending out?

7

SETTLING THE DEAL

'No question is ever settled, until it is settled right.'
Poem by Ella Wheeler Wilcox

You are now at a point where you are close to agreement in your negotiation. You will remember that this is a danger point, when it is tempting to give away your hard-earned advantage in the closing moments in order to finalise a deal. Naturally, you must be on your guard against having to make last-minute concessions.

Remember also that if you are very happy with the deal you have won, you shouldn't show it. Instead, keep a poker face. Be gracious and let the other side believe it is *they* who have been the skilful bargainers. We all need our self-respect.

CONFIRMING THE DEAL

When agreement has been reached after a complex negotiation, it is vital to confirm that both parties have actually agreed to the same deal. Misunderstandings, even at this stage, can arise all too easily with the best will in the world.

If you are inclined to be devious, you may believe it is in your best interests sometimes to settle a deal that is intentionally ambiguous. This cannot be applauded because, as we have already emphasised, the foundation of a successful negotiation should be mutual trust. However, it would be naïve to believe that some people might not be tempted to engage in such deception on occasions. Even if you do not intentionally seek an ambiguous outcome, it is always possible that the other side might. To ensure that this does not happen, and in any event as a matter of good practice, you should both formally 'agree what you have agreed'.

This should be done by writing down all the key points that you have agreed, with the corresponding conditions which are to be attached. Don't take *anything* for granted! You may well not want to produce a final legally-binding contract at this time, if this is what you were discussing, but you should sign an Agreement Subject to Contract or a Protocol (a summary of key points that have been agreed). In some countries, especially in Eastern Europe, you will find that in any event this is standard practice. If you haven't drafted this summary yourself, the final document is well worth checking, just to be sure that everything is in order. You will be asked to sign this and you will want to be certain that it does actually reflect *your* position, fully and accurately.

It is worth noting in passing, that this confirmation stage is also known as 'ratification' to many negotiators. While this is popularly understood to mean confirmation of the negotiation, in fact it has a more specific meaning in law, which relates to the principle of confirming the authority of an agent. It is thus a term better reserved to its formal legal usage, if you want to avoid any possible misunderstandings during a commercial deal.

CONTRACTUAL CONSIDERATIONS

Now for a warning! The rest of this chapter relates to commercial negotiation specifically, because the formal legal considerations can be so much more important and complex than in most other types of negotiation. However, those who are involved in buying or selling should only be prepared to ignore these contractual considerations at their peril!

In most countries' law, a commercial contract exists where an offer is made by one party and accepted by another. The offer or acceptance can be in writing, by word of mouth, partly in writing and partly by word of mouth, or it may even be implied from the conduct of the parties. (Note, however, that an 'invitation to treat' is *not* an offer in this sense. For example, a shopkeeper may display goods for sale in his shop window at a certain price, but it is well established in English law, for example, that the shopkeeper is not obliged to sell at that price – or at all.)

Many disputes could have been settled long before they ever went to law, if only both parties had spent more time setting out and up-dating their formal Terms and Conditions for sale or purchase. Of course, you need to ensure that these were attached to all your correspondence relating to Enquiries, Quotations, Orders, Acknowledgements of Orders and Invoices, as relevant to your case. This may lead to a disagreement, which will have to be negotiated, as to *whose* terms and conditions will apply. However, it is far better to resolve such matters *before* the contract is signed, rather than after the agreed transaction has taken place.

When negotiating a contract, its legal standing is a fundamentally important consideration. An 'illegal' contract, however that may be defined, is not legally enforceable. It is not therefore a valid defence to say that you did not realise it was illegal; as the law states, *Ignorantia juris neminem excusat* – Ignorance of the law is no excuse.

In negotiating any contract, you will presumably wish to set off from the beginning with the intention of making it binding upon all sides. To do this, the contract will therefore have to be *legally enforceable*. For overseas contracts, it is important to add a clause that will ensure that the agreement will be subject to a judgement that can indeed be enforced legally, if necessary. This will usually mean that you will want to state in the contract that the 'Proper Law of the Contract' shall be that relating to your own country. Otherwise, you will be dependent upon another country's statutes and case law, which might be difficult for you to ascertain in advance, and expensive to apply.

Let us now assume that you have been negotiating a contract of supply. It could be for a product, a service, or both. You might be contracting with a customer or perhaps a distributor.

In many cases you should get expert legal help and, on such occasions, you will probably have had your lawyer(s) present at the negotiations, if the matters to be discussed are in any way complex or likely to be legally sensitive. Remember, it is much better to involve your lawyer at the *beginning* of a complex

When in doubt, consult a lawyer!

contract, rather than to wait until after you have found out you are in dispute.

The following are some of the points that you will want to ensure are properly covered when your contract negotiations are finished. They will probably include

(1) a Preamble, (2) the Scope of the Contract, (3) Delivery, (4) Price, (5) the Term of Payment, (6) any Technical Documentation and/or Training, (7) Guarantees or Warranty, (8) Force Majeure, (9) Arbitration, (10) Premature Termination.

[Note: In many countries, the law relating to consumer purchases (i.e., for private use or consumption, purchased by someone 'who does not make the contract in the course of business nor pretend to') is different from business purchases. In general, 'the Public' have greater security, partly because they are seen to have less room for negotiation against a supplying company. Consumer purchases are therefore not covered in the discussion that follows.]

1 Preamble

Here, you should describe the general information relating to the contract. If either side refers to earlier tender documents or quotations in the final contract, whether explicitly or implicitly, make sure that you are happy with all that is contained there, including the General Conditions (i.e., what is sometimes known as the 'small print'). State also:

* Who you are, and where.

* Who the other party is, and where.

* Details of any other parties also involved in the contract.

* Where the contract is to be executed.

* The date and place of the agreement.

2 Scope

This section describes exactly what is to be included in the contract, and what is not. Usually the following points would be covered:

119

* What the supplier is to deliver and the quantities.

* The constituent components.

* The specifications and performance-rating of each constituent and the overall package.

* The detail of whether any sub-contracting is to be allowed and if so, where and by whom.

* What else may be involved, such as commissioning, training, etc.

* The country under which the law of the contract is to be governed, i.e., 'The Proper Law of the Contract'.

* A statement of when ownership (i.e. 'Property in the Goods') and risk is to pass. (Normally, goods remain at the risk of the seller until the property in them is transferred to the buyer, unless specifically agreed otherwise. However, when the property in the goods is transferred to the buyer, the goods are then at the buyer's risk, whether delivery has been made or not. But note an important exception to this: If delivery is delayed due to the fault of one of the parties, the goods are at the risk of that party at fault, as far as any loss is concerned which might not have occurred but for such a fault.) Responsibilities for insuring the goods might also therefore be covered in this section, if not later.

* Any exclusions or limitations of liability (noting that in many countries, many of the exclusions you might wish to make are not legally enforceable).

3 Delivery

'Time is of the essence' will be a phrase that will please few suppliers and will no doubt have been uppermost in their minds when planning their negotiation. In UK law (The Sale Of Goods Act, 1979) time will only 'be of the essence' of the contract, whether as to payment or delivery, if it is mutually agreed in the contract. Thus, there is no legal obligation to accept this, although commercially you may find it rather more difficult to avoid. Acceptance of this, with regard to delivery, will usually carry with it some form of liquidated damages (see later). These could be heavy, especially if past delivery performances have been poor, or if the contract is in any way time-sensitive. This is therefore particularly fertile ground for strong negotiators. Questions to be resolved in this section of the contract will typically include:

* What is the period of delivery, starting from when? If the offer of delivery was not for a specific date, but quoted in weeks for example, are these calendar weeks or working weeks? Note that UK law specifies that 'months' are calendar rather than lunar months, where there is doubt. (This is often a point of dispute with contracts of employment, in calculating the period of notice required of an employee who wishes to leave early).

* Is there to be any phasing of delivery? Will part shipments be allowed, for example?

* What is the place of delivery? This could be anything from 'ex supplier's works' through to 'delivered, duty and taxes paid, customer's works'. Most of the popular variations, including 'Free Alongside Ship' (FAS), 'Free On Board' (FOB), and 'Cost, Insurance and Freight' (CIF), are legally defined by 'INCO Terms' ('International Chamber of Commerce'; the latest terms at the time of writing date from 1980), to which some reference should usually be made.

* Who is to pay for the insurance, for what, when and how much? Some countries will even specify by whom (as they will possibly also specify who is to effect the carriage).

* Are part shipments or trans-shipments to be allowed? This will affect the drawing up of a letter of credit, for example.

* Is there to be some form of outside inspection of the goods before shipment or passing over of title? If so, the customer will want to demand reasonable access to the works and the goods; the supplier will want to ensure that inspection causes no undue delay after notification of readiness.

* What form of packaging is to be used? This section will usually include comment on its specification, and will perhaps specify maximum unit weights to ensure ease of handling, resistance to specific climatic conditions, etc.

* How are the goods and packages to be marked?

* What are the consequences of failure to deliver on time? If time has been

121

made the essence of the contract, there will be some statement of these consequences, and this may even include a provision for cancellation (see later). Cancellation may or may not include payment for work done (covered by the phrase *Quantum Meruit*, or 'as much as he has earned'), and could also demand the release of work completed, special tools, jigs, fittings, etc, depending on who it is agreed shall have the property in these items.

There is a point to be noted regarding 'penalty clauses' and 'liquidated damages'. These terms are frequently used, but improperly understood, by commerical negotiators. *Liquidated damages* are damages that can be assessed before a dispute goes to Court. Sums which are *not* 'a genuine pre-estimate of the damage' incurred by the injured party may be *penalties* which might not be enforceable. This is determined by applying a remarkable legal concept which prohibits holding a party *In Terrorem* (literally, 'in terror'): unreasonable claims for damages will be struck out by most courts around the world, on the basis that an injured party should not obtain damages greater than any loss reasonably arising from the actions of an offending party. Liquidated damages are usually stated in the form of an agreed percentage of the contract value per week of lateness, to a given maximum, and should be highly negotiable. Arguments you will hear at this stage of the negotiation will usually run something like the following:

Buyer: 'We want a penalty clause in order to stress how important prompt delivery is for us. Whatever we charge, it won't cover our costs. We propose . . .'

OPTION A

Seller: 'Naturally we have full confidence in our ability to supply on time. However, we do not want to be in a position where we complete the contract satisfactorily, but delivery is delayed by you. You might change your specifications, for example, or say that you cannot accept delivery at the due time when we are ready to ship. We would therefore propose the following: if any delay can be shown to be our fault, we would consider paying you some form of liquidated damages. However, if the delay is due to your actions, you must then pay us.'

122

OPTION B

Seller: 'Of course we could accept some form of liquidated damages, if we are late. However, if you were to insist upon that, we should have to demand a similar premium for each week that we were able to supply *ahead* of schedule.'

There will then be a number of variables to debate: when should the liquidated damages start to accrue? (i.e., will there be a grace period?) How much is to be payable, how often, and to what maximum? As a subsidiary issue, you may as a supplier have to consider whether damages are also to be paid for the interest lost on the delayed payments to your agents or distributors, for example.

4 Price

People new to negotiating often think that price is the key part of any deal, but of course it is only one of many important points. However, it is sometimes the easiest item to measure in terms of the cost of concessions given. Hence it is often the most sensitive.

Many buying teams are rewarded for reducing their company's outlay on a given range of items compared with the equivalent expenditure in the previous year. With their bonus in mind, they will indeed consider price a most important issue. Sales teams will naturally wish to remind such cost-sensitive buyers that security of supply and performance are also vital considerations.

Similarly, many sales people find that giving concessions on price is the easiest way to secure a deal. This may be so, but they in turn will need to be reminded that 5 per cent given away on a project with an initial gross margin of 20 per cent, for example, means that a quarter of all the available profit has been lost!

If you are in any doubt about this, consider the following worked example: Your contract is worth £100,000. If your costs in total amount to £80,000, your profit margin is £20,000 (divided by £100,000 × 100 = 20 per cent gross margin).

You now give 5 per cent away in concessions so your price is now £95,000 (£100,000 less 5/100 × £100,000), and your profit only £15,000 (£95,000 − £80,000). Your profit has therefore come down from £20,000 to £15,000, i.e. a quarter.

Contractually, some of the considerations on price should include statements clarifying the following points:

* Specifically what is included in the price (and perhaps what is *not* included).

* Whether or not the price is fixed. If not, what indices of raw material, power, labour, etc. will govern price variations, and within what time frame. Many suppliers find that this can be a fruitful area in which to increase the profitability of a deal, but your over-riding concern should normally be 'fairness' or further negotiations may well be called later on to redress the buyer's grievances.

* The currency of the contract should be stated, and whether any variations in price are to be permitted should the relevant exchange rates move. If interest is involved (e.g., for extended credit, as a penalty for late payment, etc.), how is it to be calculated? Usually a reference point will be used, such as the London Inter-Bank Rate (LIBOR), plus an agreed number of percentage points premium or discount.

* There will usually be some comment here, if relevant, on any price discount or premium (a percentage sum, usually, to be deducted from or added to a list price, in order to calculate the actual amount that is to be invoiced, and thus paid. This might perhaps be in consideration for the volume of business concerned, or for a particularly onerous product-specification or inspection requirement).

* Comment should also be made on any rebate that might be agreed. (i.e., a sum to be paid back to the customer *after* invoicing. This might be dependent, for example, on the eventual business placed in total with the supplier over an agreed period, or the actual delivery performance achieved, or some other event that cannot be quantified at the time the contract is negotiated). Rebates are especially popular with buyers in larger companies, where any refund is paid to the purchasing team's cost-centre, rather than that of the colleague who actually used the goods or service in question. This of course helps the purchasing team's bonus performance. Note that if rebates are to be calculated in varying amounts dependent upon the eventual volume of goods required by the customer, for example, it is important to state whether any given rebate, which will usually be stated as a percentage, is to be applied to the

marginal increase in volume achieved, or applicable across the *entire* contract volume. If a rebate is to be paid, the contract should also state when and how.

* On some special occasions, the price might to some degree reflect the commercial exclusivity of the deal. If exclusivity is granted by the buyer (e.g., sole supplier status), mention needs to be made of that fact, with provisions in case of failure to supply. If it is the seller who is offering exclusivity of supply, mention also needs to be made, assuming of course that the Proper Law of the Contract permits this.

5 Terms of Payment

This is an excellent area in which to test out your negotiating skills. As a buyer, you will want to hold out for paying as late as possible, with some of the payment perhaps withheld until some considerable time after delivery to ensure that commissioning is fully completed, and perhaps until later, after the initial operating performance has been proven. As a seller, however, you will seek the earliest possible payment – cash with order if possible. Some of the issues you will want to keep in mind are:

* When payment is to be made, to whom and how. Are payments to be net of local taxes, and if so, what are they? What happens if the customer delays payment? Perhaps a clause should be added to provide that the supplier may then charge interest on the sums overdue.

* Whether payment is to be guaranteed, for example by Bill of Exchange, Letter of Credit, etc. If a Letter of Credit is to be used, will it be irrevocable, confirmed by a nominated bank? If not, payment might not be enforceable.

* Whether stage payments are to be made, and if so when and against which eventualities (e.g., on receipt of raw materials, after final inspection, after despatch, after commissioning, etc.).

* Whether any of the payment is to be withheld against a performance guarantee. If so, as a supplier, can you negotiate with your client that the interest arising from the sums withheld is payable to you?

* If an agent's commission is involved, you will probably want to ensure that payment is only made to the agent after you have been paid

125

(specifying exactly how long after). You will also want to ensure that there is no ambiguity concerning the definition of how the calculation of commission is to be made (if a percentage, for example, a percentage of what?)

6 Technical Documentation and Training

This is an area where both parties might have quite fixed ideas. The following are some of the issues to be resolved and dealt with in the contract:

* Are working drawings to be provided, when, and who will hold the proprietorial right (e.g., possibly patents or registered designs) to these drawings?

* Is the proprietorial right enforceable? Many Original Equipment Manufacturers have been accustomed to making attractive profits from the supply of spare parts, but recent changes in copyright law in the UK may change this. Nevertheless, the customer may need to negotiate the prices of spare parts as part of the contract, if they are unobtainable from anyone else. If special castings are involved, for example, who will pay for the patterns (usually the customer!) and who will actually have ownership of them? This should be specified in the contract. The same considerations will apply to special jigs and tooling. If the contract is with a distributor or agent, you may especially wish to make some provision here about the rights to the use of trademarks and names applying to your product. Failure to cover this aspect can be very costly.

* Details of what instruction manuals are required, and when, should be included. Specify what is to be covered by these, how many copies will be required, and in what language they are to be written. As a supplier, you may well wish to apply an exclusion or limitation clause with regard to your liability for what these manuals advise.

* If training is to be given, state by whom, where, and for what period (this is more precise than stating for 'how long'). Identify also who will be responsible for all the related costs of this (including insurance, transport and accommodation).

* What will be the cost if additional training is subsequently found to be necessary? Will it be a condition of the contract to supply this if requested, and under what terms?

126

Inevitably, there is more to these questions than initially meets the eye. As you will now have realised, there is plenty of scope for negotiation, even in this section of a contract, which is often added (wrongly) as an after-thought.

7 Warranty

This is a subject that requires careful legal definition, although from personal experience, I have to admit that it is rarely understood fully by commercial negotiatiors who have had no legal training.

First, it is important to differentiate between a *condition*, a *guarantee*, and a *warranty*. The distinctions in law are as follows:

* A breach of a *condition* of a contract (which may be either express or implied) can repudiate that contract and give rise to damages as well.

* A *guarantee* is an example of a condition, the breach of which can result in repudiation of the contract and a claim for damages.

* A *warranty*, however, unlike a guarantee, is *not* fundamental to a contract. While it also can be express or implied, and if unfulfilled can result in damages, *it cannot result in repudiation of the contract.*

You will see therefore that 'warranty' is not a helpful term to use if you are the customer, although you will still find the term used in many Contracts of Purchase or Supply.

We should also be aware of the dangers and effects of *misrepresentation*, which might be *fraudulent*, *negligent* or *innocent* in legal terminology:

* If a contract is induced by a *fraudulent* misrepresentation (which means that the misrepresentation of a 'fact' was made dishonestly, for example with an attempt to deceive), the injured party may 'affirm' the contract and sue for damages for the deceit, or rescind the contract (with or without damages).

* If, however, the party making the misrepresentation believed that they were making a true statement of fact, the misrepresentation is *innocent*. In such circumstances, damages may not be payable, unless the injured

party can claim, for example, that the misrepresentation was made in the form of a condition or warranty, or was made *negligently* (i.e., carelessly). However, the contract may still be rescinded if the injured party can show that he did not accept the innocent misrepresentation implicitly, that he acted promptly, that no innocent third parties obtained rights in the matter for value (i.e., some form of payment), and that the parties can be restored 'to their former position'.

Regarding a guarantee of a product, in practice it will sometimes be difficult for either side to know or to prove what has constituted 'fair wear and tear', what might have been due to customer abuse, and what was due to an unreasonable failure or shortcoming of the product. These points must be kept in mind when considering and defining what the contractual obligations of each party shall be. Here are some guidelines for defining these obligations:

* State exactly what is to be covered by the guarantee (are there to be separate conditions for the spare parts supplied with the contract?), under what circumstances, and for how long. Is the guarantee null and void if the customer interferes with the goods (for instance by making necessary but unsupervised repairs or modifications?) This is the clause that many suppliers will also want to invoke if the customer uses unauthorised or unapproved spare parts – assuming it has been agreed that he may do so.

* Who is to decide if the guarantee has not been met, and how? Maybe an outside inspector should be agreed upon, in which case who is to pay for this and what should then be inspected? Indeed, what *can* be inspected?

* What will be the damages for non-fulfilment of the guarantee? Will any remedial options be allowed, and if so, who should be allowed the exercise of these options? (e.g., repair, replacement, redesign or financial redress for lost output, etc.) If repair or replacement is acceptable, is the guarantee period to be extended, and if so, for how long?

* Are consequential damages to be allowed, limited or excluded? If they are to be allowed, are they to be physical or financial? Should there be a duty to insure against such damages, and if so, on whom and for how much?

8 Force Majeure

This is the great escape clause, which will say something similar to the following:

The Party shall not be in breach of the contract in the event of any delay or any non-performance of its obligations hereunder where the delay is due to any cause beyond the Party's control. In such event, the parties may terminate or suspend this contract with no liability for loss or damage thereby occasioned.

The following shall, without prejudice to the generality of the above, be considered causes beyond the Party's control: Acts of God such as typhoon, flood or fire; war or threat of war; sabotage; insurrection; civil disturbance; requisition; Governmental restriction; prohibitions or enactments of any kind; import or export regulations; strikes; lock-outs; trade disputes (whether involving employees of the Party or another); difficulties in obtaining labour, fuel, machinery, information, data or knowhow; breakdown in machinery; accident; shipwreck or unavailability of vessels or transport; defaults by a third party.

Note that anyone relying on a Force Majeure clause, or any other exclusion, will have to bear the burden of proof that it applies in a particular instance, if for example there was any ambiguity.

Some industries have, over the years, agreed some standard clauses that are accepted to be fair and reasonable by both sides. The important points here are that:

* Such a clause should always be included in the contract, unless very special circumstances apply.

* If each side has a standard clause on Force Majeure which is different, the first question will be whose conditions will prevail. If this cannot be agreed, at the very least the Force Majeure clause adopted should be applicable equally to both parties.

* Some of the events covered by a Force Majeure clause may be insurable. Perhaps this should be a requirement of one of the parties, in which case it should be stated.

It is worth commenting on a particular phrase that you will find in nearly every Force Majeure clause: 'Acts of God'. As a general event, such 'acts' are meaningless to an insurance company unless defined (although most insurers will, nevertheless, be quite content to offer cover. The onus will be on you, the insured, to prove when such an event occurs that it was indeed an 'Act of God'. No-one to date, so far as I am aware, has yet brought a successful claim. . . .)

9 Arbitration

This is a fairly common part of a contract. However, it could be (perhaps more often than not) that you will be better and more effectively covered by the laws of the country governing the contract. In some countries, the remedies applied by the judicial system can be cheaper, and the limits applied may well be tighter, than those provided by an external arbitrator.

In any event, it is clearly important to agree what should happen in the case of a dispute. With the best will in the world, differences in opinion or interpretation of what has been agreed can arise. At the beginning of the contract, you will have agreed under which country's law the contract has been struck (the Proper Law of the Contract), and this will usually (but not always) determine where arbitration is to be governed.

You need to agree the method by which an arbitrator is to be chosen, assuming that one is indeed to be appointed. Note that it is preferable to limit the number to one in most cases, for the sake of both convenience and cost. The person chosen will usually be someone selected as being acceptable by a body which both parties agreed to nominate, such as a learned institution, or perhaps a Chamber of Commerce. (Quite often, international contracts will specify that the arbitrator should be appointed according to the Rules and Conditions of the International Chamber of Commerce.) Having agreed this, the decision of the appointed arbitrator will be final, subject of course to the legal jurisdiction of the Proper Law of the Contract. Note, however, that an arbitrator cannot be imposed after the signing of a contract, if none has been agreed beforehand. It is also worth noting that if one side has no assets that can be 'attached' by the country of the Proper Law of the contract, the judgement, whether made by an arbitrator or a court, may be unenforceable.

10 Premature Termination

Having gone to all this trouble, it might be galling to think that the contract might be terminated prematurely by one party, against the wishes of the other. Indeed, when negotiating contracts of sale, supply, employment, or even appointment as an agent or distributor, it may seem to be in very bad faith to start discussing what should happen if it all goes wrong. Nevertheless, you should, and it is very bad practice not to. It is far better to resolve such matters of principle in harmony, before a dispute occurs, rather than after.

The general details of what should happen under such circumstances will normally be covered by the Proper Law of the Contract. There may well be areas where you might wish to make special provisions, which are agreeable to both sides. If this is the case, then you should state what these are and take legal advice as to whether they are likely to be legally enforceable. There is little point in adding them to a contract if they are not, especially when discussing an event such as termination, which is itself likely to be under dispute should it ever arise.

The suggestions in this chapter are not designed to be exhaustive or complete. As you probably will have already decided for yourself, contractual matters require specialised advice, which will take into account all the details and circumstances that will apply to your specific case. (This will be especially important when the Proper Law to be applied is that of an alien country or culture.) Therefore, in such matters, let your watchword be:

Whenever in doubt, consult a lawyer!

Summary

- Leave the other side thinking that *they* have won a good deal.

- When you have reached a settlement, make sure that what you think you have agreed is the same as what the other party thinks they have agreed: in other words, confirm the agreement, and consider employing a lawyer to help you if you are in doubt.

- If you are asked to sign an Agreement subject to contract or a Protocol not drafted by yourself, make sure it states what you think has been agreed before you sign it.

- If you are negotiating a contract, decide if it needs to be binding. Presumably it will be, in which case you need to ensure that it will be legally enforceable.

- Of all the contractual considerations, one of the most important is to agree what will be the Proper Law of the Contract. There could be major problems ahead if it is not that of a country (or state) with whose laws you are familiar.

- The next most important consideration is that your own Standard Terms and Conditions, which should have been associated with your negotiations, whether for a sale or for a purchase, are up to date, fully reflect your company's trading policies, and cover all the usual clauses and contingencies.

- Where damages are to be applied, they need to be 'reasonable' if they are to be enforceable.

- A 'Warranty' is not legally a Condition of a Contract. If you want it to be, then it should be termed a 'Guarantee'.

Useful Exercise

- Now check your company's Standard Terms and Conditions of supply and purchase. Do you approve of them? If not, get them redrafted by a lawyer!

8

IMPROVING THE OUTCOME

'Power corrupts, but lack of power corrupts absolutely.' *Adlai Stevenson*

How can the outcome of any negotiation be improved? Personal experience suggests, and published research confirms, that three key qualities – and the degree to which a negotiating team possesses them – govern the success or otherwise of almost any negotiation. These are *skills*, the major subject of this book as a whole; *aspiration*, the motivating force that inspires us to go for the best outcome we can possibly win; and *power*, the major theme of this chapter.

The consistent building of a strong power-base is often what distinguishes successful negotiators from the rest. Now, without denying the importance of this, you might suspect that producing a consistent record of success may be highly dependent upon choosing carefully *when* to negotiate. In particular, when there is not a strong platform on which to build a case, you might believe that it is preferable to avoid negotiating at all, rather than run the risk of losing.

This is a variation on the 'never start an argument you cannot win' school of thought, and it is actually rather defensive. Strong positions in a negotiation are *not* pre-ordained facts of life; a power-base can be constructed, modified and even neutralised by truly skilful players.

135

POWER

First, there are some broad observations to be made about power. In the context of negotiating, it is defined as 'the capacity to influence another party', and is invariably a major consideration when looking at how the outcome of any negotiation can be improved.

This definition may appear to indicate that using power is highly manipulative. Indeed it can be; however, a curious feature of power is that it is rather like money: when you have it, you don't always need to use it, but life without it can be tough (and may be impossible).

Further, even if you have power, it is of little advantage if it is not perceived by the other side. Thus power is rarely an absolute commodity: it is relative to the other side's perception, and also to their circumstances. What makes you powerful in some situations may be quite irrelevant in others.

If the other party is *not* prepared to see things your way, you may well have to demonstrate your power-base overtly. In win-lose negotiations especially, it may therefore be necessary to wield your power by employing sanctions. Even when you prefer to aim for a win-win outcome, however, a strong power-base will clearly help tacitly to reinforce your position and strengthen your case.

With a strong power-base, polished negotiating skills become relatively less important if the will to develop high aspiration is also there. Thus, even if you are relatively new to the negotiating techniques we have discussed in preceding chapters, you can still expect a good outcome. Conversely, no matter how strong your personal bargaining skills may be, you will always need to attend to any potential weaknesses in your case.

With these thoughts in mind, let us look at how the balance of power is to be assessed, and how a power-base should be built up. This power-base might be real, or it might only be perceived (i.e. apparent to the other side but not necessarily real); it does not matter which, as long as it assists you to influence the other side.

Power may be real or perceived.

ASSESSING POWER

One of the curious features of power is that, more often than not, negotiating parties tend to believe that they have *less* power than is actually the case. Often, this is *not* because they feel that their

137

own case is necessarily weak, but because they believe wrongly that the *other* side is stronger. It is so easy to fall into the trap of believing the other side's propaganda!

A key to understanding this curious lack of confidence is to ask a sales force, their competition and their customers, just what are believed to be the relative strengths of the two competing companies. Normally, of course, this is not possible for those directly involved. However, whenever you have the chance to take up an independent position such as market researcher, trainer or consultant, a unique opportunity exists to compare each side's perceptions against reality, from a privileged and objective vantage point.

Observation of this kind often shows that sales forces underestimate their employer's actual market position and product strengths. All too readily they list advantages which they think the competition holds but believe that they themselves do not. These perceptions nearly always prove to be exaggerated, or just plain wrong. Often, the sales team have believed their customers and competitors, rather than their own market research. Similarly, buying teams rarely judge the market to be as competitive as it truly is, and often perceive that they have much less choice of supplier than is actually the case. All too often, it appears, negotiating teams *over*estimate the strength of the other side.

Normally, of course, it is rare for any of the participants to know the real balance of power between two or more teams. The only way to be sure is to *test reality* and do so often. Thus, wise buyers will not always buy from what is, apparently, the cheapest source. Similarly, experienced sales managers realise that they have to be prepared to lose business sometimes by being overpriced, just so they can be sure that they know what the real market price-level is.

REAL POWER

What conditions or circumstances can enhance the intrinsic strength of a negotiating position? Perhaps the best situation, if you can arrange it, will be one that takes advantage of this basic principle:

The less you appear to have to gain by agreeing or disagreeing to a deal, the stronger you will in fact be.

The more the other side believe that you may have no real need to negotiate, the greater will be the concessions that they will feel they must give you, in order to persuade you to conclude a deal.

Conversely, if the other side can see that in fact there are rich prizes for *you* to win or lose during a negotiation, your power-base will be substantially diminished. They will then reason that because the deal will be so much more important to you than to them, you will naturally be prepared to give up more in order to achieve your objectives. In these circumstances, the other party will try to exploit your position to the full, by extracting as many valuable concessions from you as possible.

Power can be won in many other ways, depending on the circumstances. It can be won by blatant use of physical or moral superiority, as may be seen in some industrial disputes and political debates, for example. Alternatively, if you are a lawyer, then obviously your case is strengthened by having convincing evidence, strong witnesses, or just the favourable precedents of case law, on your side.

In commerce, however, power is gained rather differently. We will look now at the main sources of commercial power, concentrating first on factors favouring those on the buying side of a negotiation.

A buyer gains strength, above all else, by having a *choice of supply*. Then, if any particular supplier wishes to deal with you, that supplier will always be weakened by having to match what others will offer, who *may* be much more hungry for business.

Less obviously, a buying team can build power over time by creating a *strong reputation*. This might be a reputation for excellence, which can be used to influence potential suppliers because it will enhance their own reputation when they sell to other companies in the same industry. Alternatively, the reputation may be for prompt payments, flexibility, or some other feature which makes this company particularly attractive to deal with. I had one customer who was well known for paying slightly more than anyone else. But whenever there was any problem, such as a product shortage, a hint of a quality problem or a query on quantities actually shipped, this customer received a service that was way beyond what anyone else achieved, without demur.

A power-base is also automatically available to a buyer who has the virtue of *size*. A threat to withdraw business then becomes much more potent, particularly to any supplier who is relatively small and consequently very dependent upon that customer. Many smaller companies refuse to deal with certain large buyers for this very reason. Refusing to deal may well put both parties in a 'win-lose' position, but it does at least save the smaller party from the risk of being squeezed later. (This refusal to deal typically arises when the large customer has acquired a reputation of not paying its smaller suppliers' bills on time.)

Note that deliberately contriving a lose-lose negotiation can also be an excellent power-builder for the next time, for it reinforces the message that you don't need to settle. It is a weapon that can be used by either the buying or the selling side.

Buyers can also exert power rather more subtly by controlling the market, for example by acquisition. This has been a particularly popular strategy for industrial enterprises in recent times, following the contraction of many of the more traditional manufacturing industries in the Western world after a decade and more of oil crisis.

A sales team gains strength by *having sole supply* of a product or service for which a demand exists or can be created. This, of course, is the goal of all marketing managers: no competition! For suppliers of spare parts and specialist 'add-on' goods, this monopolising of supply is indeed widely practised, although it depends upon being able to enforce proprietorial ownership over design copyright, patents, or whatever.

Alternatively, a supplier can aim for a *superior product or service*, which will offer the customer benefits and advantages that no other supplier can match. (This is naturally what *all* sales people would like their customers to believe!) If this isn't possible, you can instead aim to have the *lowest cost-base and/or the lowest price*.

There are other possibilities for enhancing power which apply in all circumstances:

Confidence. You can increase your personal power simply by having very high confidence in yourself and your position. In part, this means being fully briefed on your own case and both sides' objectives – i.e., being well prepared. High confidence also means *ignoring the apparent status or power of the other side*, as if it were of no importance or relevance to you. You are therefore more prepared to trade concessions reluctantly, if at all, and move in smaller steps.

Diversion. Sometimes you can gain power by diversion. This means side-tracking the discussion away from your sensitive areas (thus neutralising the other side's strength), towards those areas where *you* are strongest (and the other side, naturally, is at its weakest).

Walking out. Being prepared to walk out is especially important, particularly against a strong adversary. Sometimes, to match strength with strength, you have to say, 'We don't want to deal with you under *those* conditions', even if you really do not mean it (because, for example, you cannot afford to do without that supplier or customer). This is where *perceived power* becomes particularly important.

PERCEIVED POWER

Sometimes, however hard you work at it, your real power-base will indeed be weak. (You can't expect to be dealt four aces *every* poker hand you play, can you?) In such circumstances, you will have to build up an *apparent* power-base which will seem strong and invincible in the mind of the other side.

The aim is to lead the other side into thinking that *you* have more power than is really the case, just as the other side will wish to work hard to make you believe it is *they* who are stronger. As we saw in Chapter 3, in the early discussion of win-lose negotiations, what people believe can be more important than the truth. It is the other side's *perceptions* that are important here, not necessarily the *reality*.

To achieve this perceived power-base, there are three kinds of tactics you can try:

1) Show imagined indifference to doing a deal. In a sense, this is *the power of brinkmanship*. If you don't receive something valuable from the other side, you must make them believe that their objectives will be at risk; that you might walk away if you don't get a better deal.

2) Be a little bit irrational sometimes. It is very difficult to negotiate against a team who concentrate on their *feelings*, without giving rational reasons for their choice of action. If you are a very rational sort of person, this tactic can be especially commended for use by you – or, for that matter, against you!

3) You may even wish to bluff, i.e., to make statements that are plausible but not true. For example, 'We are not interested in dealing with you unless you pay cash with order,' or 'We have a bid here for the same specification that you have offered at a somewhat cheaper price than your quotation'.

As far as building a power-base is concerned (leaving conscience aside for the moment), it does not matter whether such statements are true, *as long as you can persuade the other side that they are.*

There are, however, other considerations regarding what might be called 'enhancing the truth'.

ENHANCING THE 'TRUTH'

There is a fine dividing line between using hints, half-truths or passive silence to persuade the other side to believe something which is not true, and actually lying (which is active). Many do tell full-blooded lies, but it is not recommended because you will usually be found out in the end. You will never be trusted again, whether you then actually tell the truth or not. We have repeatedly stated that *personal integrity* (as gauged by past performances) is a major requirement for success as a negotiator. Without integrity, your power-base will rarely influence anyone because it will not be credible.

However, this is a practical book, so it must be acknowledged that some negotiators do appear to feel that there are different sorts of lies and 'untruths', some being more acceptable than others. (Indeed, most people would say that, from personal experience, few if any negotiators appear to feel constrained to tell the *whole* truth, all of the time.) It might therefore be helpful to see what some famous people have said on the subject.

Samuel Butler is recorded as saying, rather wittily, 'I do not mind lying, but I hate inaccuracy.' This might perhaps be the motto of the 'Don't Get Found Out' school of thought! (Incidentally, not being 'found out' was also reputed to be the second of two unspoken Laws of the Boy Scouts, the first being that a Scout is no fool. You might think that both of these are quite useful rules for negotiators, too.)

Actually, not everyone expects to hear the whole truth all the time anyway; this view is expressed rather pragmatically by H. L. Mencken: 'It is hard to believe that a man is telling the truth, when you know that you would lie if you were in his place.'

The acceptability or otherwise of lying, or more generously termed, bluffing and gilding the lily, is best left to readers and their consciences. Perhaps the most helpful comments come from the Earl of Chesterfield:

'There are some occasions when a man must tell half his secret, in order to conceal the rest.'
'A man who tells nothing, or tells all, will equally have nothing told him.'

Revealing *and* concealing your position simultaneously is one of the more demanding skills of a good negotiator. This means that trust has to be established, for example, by an exchange of truthful information, but not to the extent that the *whole* of your case is ever revealed. Thus, you might well say 'Your price was not acceptable' quite honestly, without needing to add that no-one else has been able to meet your technical specifications or delivery times.

ABUSE OF POWER

Before we move on, it is worth considering one potential trap. The greater the power you possess, the more dangerous can be its abuse.

With power goes the potential for coercion. Sometimes you will *want* to coerce, for example in a win-lose power-play. The inherent danger is that the other side may see a display of naked power as something best avoided, by refusing to deal at all. You will then have converted your win-lose into lose-lose.

In order to avoid this, split your negotiating duties into two parts. The first will be *task* oriented. You have some objectives to achieve: plan accordingly. *Then add another consideration.* Think of the *people* you are dealing with. What effect will your high power-base have on them? Might you frighten them off? If so, coercion is clearly inadvisable.

If you are not sure about this, ask yourself if you have ever had a strong position in the past which has still produced a poor result for you. It may have seemed at the time that it was the other side's fault: they just wouldn't do things your way. It is possible that they were only mirroring your aggressive style, as the only defence they had available to them in the circumstances.

This is a hard lesson to learn, but a valuable one. The apparently slow, unexcitable negotiators will rarely let a high power-base be an obstacle to success. Why should they? They know full well that the other side will have to come round to their way of thinking in due course. The hungry, aggressive 'tigers' will, in contrast, frequently frighten their quarry away before they can ever get close enough to savage, maul and take their prize.

The secret is to sit back, relax, and take your time. Even if your power-base is unassailable, no matter how you eventually choose to use it you can always afford to *invest time in building up trust.* You may actually end by saying, 'Don't be unreasonable! Do it my way,' but only after you have first gently persuaded the other side that this is the right and logical thing for them to do.

Echoing this sentiment, an American colleague of mine used to say: 'I like to stand beside people and slip into their pocket before they even know I am there.' It may appear to be a devious tactic, but it never seemed that way at the time and it always worked very well for him; he never frightened *his* quarry away. Thus, a warm reception and an initial friendly greeting is infinitely preferable to a gruff 'Sit down and listen to what I am going to tell you' approach. *First impressions are very important.*

Further, reconsider the points made in Chapter 3 about arguing. In particular, don't sledgehammer the other side's case with your opposition too soon. Use *logical persuasion*: build your case up with undeniable logic before drawing the inevitable conclusion.

POWER – ASPIRATION – SKILL

Having explored power in a little more detail, it is important to put it into context with the other requirements of a successful negotiator: aspiration and skill. What happens when all three requirements are *not* blended together?

High power, unskilled and on its own, may not be very profitable in the long term, especially if the power-base is abused, as we have seen. Such negotiators become rather like the school bully; no-one wants to play with them. Note also that when such negotiators do find someone to 'play' with, their greater power may still be nullified by a skilled performer with high aspiration. This last statement has been demonstrated by controlled experiments, which also reveal another interesting finding. Unskilled negotiators *do* improve when they have more power, as one would expect, but skilled negotiators do not. In other words, the difference in performance between skilled and unskilled negotiators decreases when both possess greater power than their respective opponents. This finding highlights just how important power is in negotiating better deals.

High skill can also be ineffectual on its own, especially if coupled with low aspiration. It is hard to imagine skilled performers not alloying their hard-earned skills with power and aspiration in order to improve their case, but it does happen. Negotiators can

145

sometimes become complacent and lazy. Be warned! A danger of complacency, highlighted by laboratory experiments, is that skilled negotiators with greater power tend to be benevolent toward unskilled opponents.

High aspiration on its own is rather different. Experience shows that negotiators with higher goals consistently achieve better results than those who aim lower. Conversely, when people have low aspirations and expect less, they usually end up with less.

Various types of negotiators can be identified who exhibit different combinations of these three most desirable features: power, skill and aspiration. For instance, you may come across the *enthusiastic amateur*, a type with low skill but high power and aspiration.

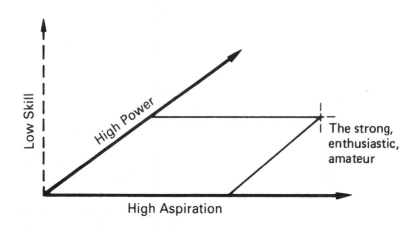

This is potentially a very powerful amalgam. Because of the low skill-base, however, such negotiators will probably miss signals and thus frequently end in deadlock. In such circumstances, they will probably need your help to avoid a sterile outcome for both parties. These occasions will require supreme strength of character and skill from you. The danger is that when you help the other side, they may seize the advantage. Then, they may WIN but your chances of LOSING could be high.

146

Alternatively, you might find yourself in the position of a *weak professional*, i.e., you may have high levels of skill and aspiration but a weak power base.

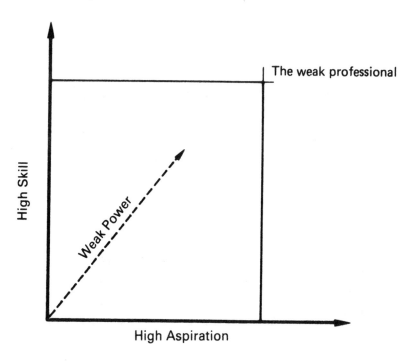

The lack of a real power-base can be a quite frequent, if rather subtle, problem. The task in hand must be to build an *apparent* power-base. Published research shows that skilled negotiators with high aspiration levels can then be big winners, regardless of whether they have *real* power or not. Indeed, in one experiment where both parties shared an *equal* power-base, *skilled performers obtained results two and a half times better than unskilled negotiators faced with the same conditions.*

High skill and power, but low aspiration, should be an impossible combination. Nevertheless, it can be found in what may be called the *demoralised professional*.

This combination can result from laziness, but more usually it is brought about by overestimating the opposition, thus failing to

147

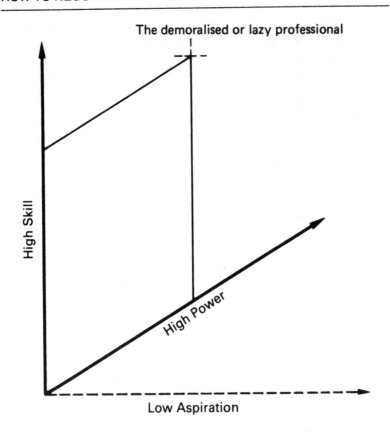

The demoralised or lazy professional

High Skill

High Power

Low Aspiration

recognise the inherent power actually contained in one's own case. The best remedy is still to aim high. This will demonstrate how strong the position really is. Time and again, experience shows that *high initial demands improve the probability of success*. As long as the initial demand is not totally unreasonable, the chances of failure or deadlock will be slight.

The strongest negotiators, then, make sure that they possess all three basic requirements, high power, high aspiration and high skill. These will indeed improve the outcome of whatever deals you have in mind.

The figure on page 149 demonstrates the various possible permutations of these requirements, which we have described, together with the ideal, which is the combination of all three. It is

148

a useful diagram to keep in mind as a conceptual check-list against which to match your position in any specific negotiation. If your first analysis does not show you that you have the optimum blend of the three basic requirements, you know that you must re-appraise the situation and remedy the missing part in order to secure the best deal possible.

The optimum blend of
POWER — ASPIRATION — SKILL

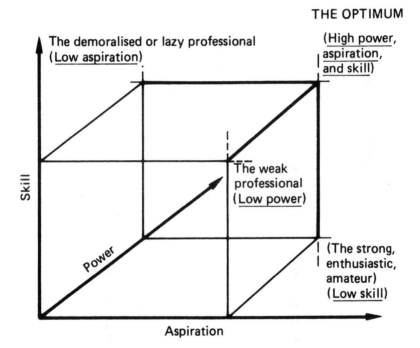

Summary

- In order to win the best result from a negotiation, a blend of three important attributes is necessary: Skill, Aspiration and Power.

- Power is the capacity to influence another party.

- It is vital to build up a power-base, whether it is real or apparent.

- A power-base can be built up by having no real need to settle, a strong market position, personal confidence, and little regard for the other side's status or power. It can be aided by being prepared to walk out of a negotiation if necessary.

- The other side's power-base will usually be over-estimated. It is therefore imperative to verify it.

- Negotiating power can be enhanced by concentrating on feelings rather than rational argument, especially when your real power-base is weak.

- Weakness can be hidden by building 'perceived power' in the mind of the other side, or by diverting them away from their strengths.

- The exercise of power requires integrity and credibility. Without them, even a strong position will not be recognised as being so.

- Nevertheless, few people will tell the whole truth, all the time. An experienced negotiator will skilfully blend revelation with concealment.

- Power can easily be abused. Be sure that weaker parties are not frightened away from the negotiating table, thus leading to a lose-lose outcome. First impressions in this respect are particularly important, aided both by building up a logical argument to support the power-base, by relaxing, and avoiding over-aggression.

- When one side has a strong power-base, the differences in performance between skilled and unskilled negotiators become smaller.

- High aspirations win higher rewards. You can help ensure this by making high initial demands.

- The optimum position, in order to negotiate the best deal, is to have high levels of power, aspiration and skill.

Useful Exercise

- Take a recent or forthcoming negotiation issue that you know of and list all the points of real power that apply to each side. (Just check how many of these *are* real.) With whom does the balance of power lie? Next, list all the areas for each side that could be turned into an apparent power-base. How can these be used to *reverse* the balance of overall strength?

9

PERSONALITY AND
CULTURAL DIFFERENCES

'All the world's a stage, and all the men and women merely
players.'
Jacques, in William Shakespeare's *As You Like It*

The aim of this chapter is to place the negotiating skills we have
discussed into the personal context in which they will be
employed. After all, in many negotiations, the personalities are
just as important as the issues. As an example of this, we have
already noted (in the section on team selection in Chapter 4) that
shared regard and warmth between teams can increase the pros-
pects of a mutually successful outcome. Equally, mistrust will
almost certainly be an obstacle.

In order to anticipate the likely responses of those we expect to
have to face, we need to understand and evaluate:

The roles the other side are likely to adopt. After all, experience
teaches that people vary as the task changes. When it comes to a
negotiation, the choice of role-model will usually be related to
the power-base and choice of negotiating style (e.g. cooperative
or competitive), as well as the position taken up in the negotiating team (e.g. leader, reviewer, surveyor, etc.). You, also, will
influence the role others adopt, through their previous experiences in meeting you, and even your initial greeting (e.g. welcoming, questioning, aggressive, defensive, etc.).

Their routine behaviour patterns, such as formal or informal, authoritarian or consultative, introvert or extrovert, etc., independent of the specific circumstances. Note that these can be quite separate from the role-model they have chosen for a particular negotiation. Sometimes there will be conflict. For example, they might have chosen a 'leadership' role-model, but may be naturally inclined to let others propose initiatives. They may want a win-win outcome, but just cannot refrain from making aggressive statements.

Their personality. This is an unfortunate word to use because, while we may all think we know what we mean by 'personality', it really defies an acceptable, universal, definition. For our purposes, however, let us assume it may be an amalgam of the selected role-model and the intrinsic behaviour patterns described above, together with individual characteristics such as: the individual's perceived needs, values and attitudes (the so-called affective aspects); the degree of will-power that an individual will use to support and defend these needs and values, when challenged by disagreement or defiance; and the intellectual attainment and cognitive aspects of an individual, such as speed and fluency of thought, the degree of tolerance for ambiguity (set against the desire for structure, certainty and 'facts'), critical reasoning ability, and so on.

Because of the importance of understanding human behaviour, you will not be too surprised to learn that a great deal of the academic research work on negotiating has been carried out by psychologists, rather than schools of management or business studies. However, even when I asked a knowledgeable friend for advice on a definition of 'personality', I was asked in return: 'What is truth? In this area there is no truth.' (And this from a professor of psychology!)

This book is therefore *not* the place to debate the matter. We can, however, usefully raise our level of awareness of some of the more important issues, such as interpersonal skills, the dangers of stereotyping, the evaluation of negotiating postures and observations on cultural differences. These are the subjects of this chapter.

INTERPERSONAL SKILLS

One of the keys to developing the ability to deal harmoniously with others must surely be a thorough understanding of ourselves. The plotting of personality profiles is a most useful tool to help us here, and tests such as the Cattell 16-PF, FIRO-B and Myers-Briggs are becoming increasingly popular aids, not only for building personal self-knowledge, but also for gaining knowledge of one's own team.

These tests might help you determine, for example, if you are an outward looking, extrovert type, and if so, whether your approach relaxes others and puts them at ease or whether it sometimes threatens those who do not appear to possess the same confidence as you. If the latter is true, it is important to know under what circumstances this can happen and how your natural enthusiasm might sometimes best be contained or restrained.

Perhaps, instead, you are a more inward, reflective person, whom others might describe as being introverted. This can be a very strong negotiating style if, underneath, you possess a confident and resilient outlook that will allow you to be assertive and directive when necessary. However, if you lack personal confidence, it is important that you learn to see yourself in a much more positive and favourable light. Otherwise, you may well be swamped by other, more forceful, people. The danger will then be that your own view of yourself, as being uncertain and low in confidence, will be further reinforced as a self-fulfilling prophecy.

Alternatively, especially if you possess a strong and formal scientific education, you might be acutely analytical in your approach to debate and discussion. This is clearly a major benefit when plotting strategy and examining options, especially if the issues are complex and interrelated. However, emotional arguments and ambiguity will, accordingly, be very difficult for such people to handle, unless they understand and are fully aware of their own attitudes and approach.

Such an analytical and rational approach may therefore clash badly with that of others on the team who adopt a more intuitive and possibly less structured attitude; they will sometimes find strictly rational argument pedantic or even counter-productive. They, in turn, need to be aware that not everyone can tune in to their wavelength. In order to win credibility, they may have to consider forcing themselves to present a more rigorously coherent analysis on occasions, at least to colleagues.

Most of us have a deep-seated desire for a degree of involvement, or *affiliation*, with our fellow human beings (and thus with the organisation they represent). However, for some people this need for belonging is so pronounced that it is difficult for them to separate issues from personalities. This needs to be guarded against. It can lead to a lack of objectivity, especially with regard to ranking priorities.

In sharp contrast to the person who must belong, there are those who exhibit very little sense of affiliation or belonging. They may well find themselves, on occasion, negotiating from a base that is considerably distant from their own side's formal position. Such individuality can produce highly constructive and imaginative solutions. In its more extreme form, however, it can be a liability to the 'home' side. It is also worth noting that such a characteristic can lead to very low regard for social or legal convention. This may clearly become counter-productive.

STEREOTYPING

As you can see from the foregoing, awareness of the effect we each have on others is a vital part of becoming a successful negotiator. We also need to be able to gauge the effect others might have on us.

Many people's attitudes and responses to given situations fall into repeatable patterns. Even as untrained but intelligent observers, it should therefore be possible for us to predict from the available evidence, often with reasonable accuracy, the problems or opportunities that might lie ahead with people and situations we have met before. This is especially useful in team-selection, where matching compatible types with their opposite numbers on the other side's team can be a powerful factor in achieving mutually beneficial deals.

156

We need to be certain, however, that we do not fall into the trap of stereotyping people. It is clear that personalities can mould jobs, but many will say that jobs can also mould personalities. The danger is that before we know it, we are tempted then to classify people by the jobs they do, rather than the specific personality traits they exhibit. Such stereotyping is bound to be very misleading.

For example, some people like to characterise buyers as inclined to being introverted. Is this true? Of course not! Buyers are just as likely to be extrovert (in order to match the wild exuberance of the 'thrusting, dynamic' sales people they meet, perhaps?). But, then, are all successful sales types forceful, independent extroverts? Some no doubt will be, but many will not. Either way, the great majority of *successful* sales people learn to keep their thoughts to themselves, keep quiet and listen hard for a large part of the time. Hardly the behaviour of a raving extrovert, you might think!

Therefore, in gauging the personalities we are going to meet in the following pages, concentrate on the evidence available to you, rather than any stereotype which might influence you (or others on your team) in your judgements.

'DIFFICULT' TYPES

Let us presume, therefore, that you have weighed up the other side as accurately as you feel the evidence available to you allows: not by job function, for example, but by their attitude and approach. Here are some of the types you might meet (indeed, you might recognise some of them!), together with some suggestions for how you might handle them:

The strong and silent types. We have already said that these people are likely to be good negotiators. Somehow, *you* do all the work and *they* reap all the benefit. Of course, such people *might* be naturally shy, quiet types. They may, alternatively, just be deliberately uncommunicative when it comes to negotiating. Usually you will not know which is the case. It could be that perhaps both statements are accurate: they *are* naturally retiring personalities, *and* they have also learnt that it often pays to say as little as possible.

Whichever is the case, you need to open such people up. Ask them questions about themselves, their business and their needs. Ask for their opinions. Engage them in conversation, and give them time and space to respond. (That means *you* need to keep quiet). When the time comes, these types of negotiators will often give good, clear signals, but you will have to listen out for them, carefully.

The strong and silent types are likely to be good negotiators.

The uninterested type. This person is an awkward variation of the strong and silent, and can be very powerful. If you meet this approach, your tactics should be the same as for the silent types: Engage them and involve them. A paper and pencil are useful tools. Sketch out the layout of a piece of equipment, draw a diagram, do some sums, or whatever, and encourage the uninterested party to lean across the table to see what you are doing. For instance, I once used a sample to capture my uninterested party's attention, when I was a 'rookie' salesman. I poured some of a new metal-working lubricant I was selling into a plastic teacup which I had spotted in the reception area. I wanted my buyer to use it. Unfortunately, the solvent in the lubricant dissolved the plastic of the container and it ran all over a polished display cabinet. When he saw what had happened, he soon became very interested in the product's possibilities. It wasn't planned, but it worked very well!

The talkers. These are a rather more unusual discovery in a negotiation, although they can be found in more straightforward deals quite regularly. If the monologue such a person presents is usefully revealing, you will have no complaint. Problems arise, however, when the talking goes on, seemingly forever, but the issues are never addressed. Every time you make a telling point, it is used as a springboard for another avalanche of frothy ideas that don't advance the discussion at all.

Talkers may neither explore nor signal. Sometimes, useful clues *can* be picked up from them, so don't rush into trying to stem the tide too soon. However, when you feel that you do need to call a halt, you will have to insist on taking a very active, directive and controlling role. To get a word in edgeways, a popular tactic is to interrupt by saying the person's name, quite forcefully. As soon as you have their momentary attention, you must call a halt, refer to the time limits you have set, and insist that the agenda be followed. This can be an ideal role for a specific member of your team, whom you effectively appoint (unilaterally) to the role of *chairman*. This person must then assume authority over what is discussed, and for how long, summarising regularly where necessary so that the debate can be redirected towards the key issues.

If the opposing side consists of more than just the talker, direct as many comments and questions as you can to other people on their team. They will be fully aware of their colleague's propensity to monopolise conversations without advancing them, and will normally be your strongest ally in neutralising the nuisance. After all, if you are not being encouraged to disclose the details of your case, they will feel that *their* position is being weakened.

The rude, the bad-tempered and the overbearing. Some people favour this approach for any negotiations they might be involved in, and they are, indeed, at least predictable. The best advice for dealing with them is *not to respond likewise.* However difficult it may be, try to stay cool, calm and polite. Do not allow yourself to be drawn into futile debate. If you are met with a torrent of invective, don't interrupt. Let it flow on and exhaust itself. If a complaint against you is made, acknowledge that you have understood what has been said, whether or not you are prepared to accept the full complaint. A powerful way of indicating that you have actually been listening is to re-state what you have just been told, perhaps asking if that was a correct summary. You might then try asking if *they* would like to repeat a particularly ill-advised phrase, if you think this might shame them into withdrawing it.

Above all, do not mirror their rude manner, ill-temper or domineering spirit. If you do, matters will go from bad to worse. Role-playing exercises regularly show that such a clash of wills invariably ends in lose-lose. (However, when I am sworn at, as a negotiating tactic, I personally like to use the same swear word in response, to demonstrate with levity that I won't be bullied: 'What do you call this xxxxing apology for an offer, then?' I might be asked. 'Oh!' I reply, smiling. 'I don't think I would call it a *xxxxing* offer.' It works quite well.)

The friendly type. These people can be just as bad, if behind their veneer of smiles you spot trouble. Some negotiators try to be everybody's friend, shying away from making decisions that might help you, but hurt someone else. This is unlikely to satisfy you and sometimes you will have to force the other party into *making choices* between what may be unpalatable options.

Alternatively, you may find that the 'friendly' opponent is only trying to lull you into a false sense of security. For example, you might be told: 'We really liked your product. In fact, we will be wanting some more soon. Unfortunately we have had a problem in the works, so you won't mind if we pay your invoice a couple of weeks late, will you?' On such occasions, you have to be firm. What you do may depend on your company's policy. You might have to use the tactic of *limited authority:* 'I'm sorry, I am afraid I don't have the power to do that.' Or, as a win-win solution to the case above, you might try saying: 'Of course not, but you do understand that we shall have to recover the cost of this somehow. Would you prefer us to invoice the cost as an interest charge to you now, or would you like to give us another order today, so that we can cover the interest costs by amending our price for this occasion?'

The busy type. This sort of negotiator is a very different problem. You cannot hold his attention for five seconds before he is interrupted by a phone-call, a knock on the door or whatever. The best solution is to ensure that negotiations do not start until you can *isolate* him from his office and other distractions. In fact, most people who fall into this category usually respond very well to sympathetic understanding: 'How on earth do you cope with all this pressure? I don't know how you do it. Don't you ever have a break?' You are now ready to make your points, taking care to propose solutions for each of the problems you have raised. Argue your case concisely and logically and you will rarely be disappointed. The busy type is not usually well prepared – he just doesn't have the time.

The wily type. This is the negotiator who is not only known to be quite skilful, he is also known to be full of tricks and ways to score points off you; perhaps the sort who some people would say gives negotiating a bad name. While this type will be no pleasure to deal with, you will be aware that this is generally a very poor style to adopt because it raises barriers of mistrust, which will usually serve only to frustrate the successful conclusion of a deal.

In the early stages, it is wise (and 'adult') to *ignore the point-scoring.* However, if mistrust becomes a significant aspect of the negotiation, it is perfectly reasonable to adopt the lessons of assertiveness training. Rather than label the offending party, as 'a trickster' perhaps, concentrate on your *feelings*: You might say, for example, 'We really would like to deal with you. But I have to say that I feel at the moment I couldn't justify to myself, or to my colleagues, any confidence that you will do what you have just promised.' This is implicitly threatening a collapse of the negotiation and even a walk-out. However wily your opponents may be, they will rarely want to prejudice the eventual deal in this way. If you believe that such a statement of your feelings has had its due effect, it can be useful to follow it up with, 'How do you think you can put our minds at rest?' The ball is now firmly in the other side's court.

The dishonest type. This negotiator is a specific variety of the wily type. What can be done, without prejudicing your own moral standards? The best way to handle outright dishonesty is to *turn a mirror towards the offending party*, so that they may see what they look like. For example, a Nigerian shopkeeper asked the publisher of this book an excessive sum for a gift he wished to buy. 'But surely, my friend,' the publisher said, 'you do not want to tarnish the good name of your country by overcharging me?' It turned out that, indeed, the shopkeeper did not!

The very senior type. This highly authoritative person can be a special joy to negotiate with. He often has everything to lose and little to gain. Try not to be overawed by being in the presence of The Great, whose 'greatness' is their strongest weapon. You will find that *strong, cogent arguments will be well received*. Be prepared to ask for their advice, if it is appropriate, but also be prepared to aim high. Concessions won from the very senior negotiator are usually very valuable and cannot be over-ruled.

The experts. This type can be difficult to negotiate against because any argument which you might adopt is a potential challenge to their professional integrity. Sometimes, it will be to your advantage to *bring in your own expert*. However, you might also be able to divert 'expert' arguments into a sideline, where they become less relevant. Concede a technical point if you have to, graciously; you may well stand an excellent chance of satisfying their needs, and yours, without having to give anything else.

Fortunately, 'experts' rarely tell lies knowingly. The strength of their case is founded upon their expertise. For this reason, make sure that your case is equally truthful and not exaggerated. They are also usually very helpful 'talkers': ask for their advice and invariably they will give it. If your discussion has a major commercial element to it, you should be able to make the other side's technical expert *your* strongest ally. This is because once you have satisfied the expert's needs, he or she won't want to see these 'gains' prejudiced by commercial considerations, which the expert will see as being less important, and possibly even damaging.

The indecisive type. You will, occasionally, come up against negotiators who just cannot make their minds up as to what they want. If you offer them a choice, they cannot decide. This is clearly a very weak negotiating style, although one that might in many circumstances give you no special advantage. The answer is to give them *few options*. Better still, try and reach their boss.

NATIONAL CHARACTERISTICS

Apart from being able to handle a variety of personality types, something for which you will of course need to prepare before a negotiation, there is also the possibility of having to accommodate different *cultural* styles. Preparation of this sort will naturally be particularly important for those with international business to conduct overseas.

Of course, there are some special difficulties that can lie ahead for you here. Just as there is the problem of trying to identify personality types, without falling into the trap of stereotyping, there is the same difficulty in trying to identify, *helpfully*, the negotiating characteristics of different cultures. Perhaps this is what Thomas Fuller had in mind when he wrote, 'Travel makes a wise man better but a fool worse.' Accurate assessments of generalities can help enormously. Inaccurate ones can only serve to confuse.

If you ask people to identify their *own* nationality's negotiating characteristics, it is rare to receive a helpful reply. (I know, because I asked many of my overseas contacts in preparing to write this book!) Of course, we are all different and in any event, national characteristics vary widely from region to region.

However, if you ask any well-travelled and experienced negotiator to tell you about the styles of *other* nationalities, invariably you will receive a very detailed description. Sometimes the replies will be prejudiced by untypical personal experiences, but often the key features of any given style described by one observer will be confirmed by others.

The question, therefore, is whether such descriptions can be helpful to you. In my experience, the answer is a definite 'Yes!' as long as these comments on cultural style are treated as being no more than broad generalisations, from which some helpful guidance can be obtained as a prelude to gaining a more specific and detailed understanding on an individual basis. In a new situation I would always prefer to have a generalised view, broad and non-specific though it might be, of the style I am likely to meet, rather than to have no awareness at all. Some information is better than none, and forewarned *is*, usually, forearmed.

The following comments are therefore offered on this basis. Check them against your own experiences and *pool the insights with your own colleagues*. What do you think? Even if you reject some of their suggestions, you might still be interested to learn what others say. After all, they might be describing you!

The British approach to negotiating has often been characterised as enthusiastic, friendly and (usually) honest. (After all, it was the British who gave the term 'fair play' to the world.) It is a style that is often commented upon by other nationalities as easy to get along with, flexible, and likely to be responsive to the other side's proposals. However, there has been criticism that this style can also be over-confident, under-prepared and naïve, reflecting the more typical characteristics of a beginner. Perhaps calling this 'the British approach' is no more than a fair reflection of the long time it has taken many North Europeans to realise that negotiating skills are actually worth cultivating.

If you fall into this category, your strengths will usually be as a cooperative, rather than competitive, negotiator. If this should be seen by the other side, your case will appear to them intrinsically weak unless you use power and aspiration well. If, by chance, you accept that you have entered deals in the past where you were under-prepared or 'taken for a ride', re-read this book, polish your skills and prepare better!

If you should have the opportunity to meet these characteristics in an adversary while negotiating, you will find a win-win style of negotiation most likely to be fruitful. You will, however, also find a win-lose prospect very attractive if you have the power-base to back it up, or even just higher aspirations.

The North American approach is seen by others to reflect the popular image of the indigenous population: good at 'wheeler-dealing', generally confident and with high aspirations for success (which the home culture is believed to reward better than most). It is also often regarded as a warm and sincere approach. In general, the American is seen to regard simplicity of both thought and action particularly highly. (You may know of the famous injunction which is said to originate from the USA: 'Keep it simple, stupid,' or 'KISS'.)

When it comes to contractual matters, there are two highly contrasting North American approaches. One, indeed, is 'simple': The over-all 'big picture' is most highly valued, to the extent that side-issues may be under-played and there will be little relish for long, detailed 'nit-picking' debate, or even formal agreements. Rather, there may be much greater reliance on the *spirit* of an agreement. (I once tried to negotiate a distributor agreement in the Mid-West. We became involved in a debate over a small, but important, detail. My opposite number refused to spend any time on it. 'Do you want to fish, or cut bait?' he asked me.)

There is another approach which is quite the opposite, however. Legal agreements may be elaborate, sometimes verbose and always expensive, to a degree that makes them exceptional. Perhaps it was this latter approach that inspired the former.

The American approach is usually recognised to be very strong in face-to-face communications, but often less so with the written word. Most foreigners find that Americans are often good bargainers, well prepared to say what *they* feel and what *they* want. (The Mexican Gulf oil market, as just one example, is particularly famed for this. 'Where are the xxxxing spare parts you promised me?' an English colleague of mine was asked by a giant 6′5″ rig supervisor, who would have looked more at home as a line-backer with the Dallas Cowboys. 'In your xxxxing ware-house,' came my colleague's reply. Fortunately, no-one seemed to take offence at this exchange and they got on together, from then on, like long-lost brothers!)

In general, while very professional themselves when negotiating, Americans are also noted for respecting professionalism in the other side. If this style or approach is close to yours, you will probably have recognised already the many strengths that you have, for high confidence is one of your many assets. For some, however, more time should be taken to pick up signals, in written communications especially, and more time should be spent developing subsidiary goals. Many foreigners remark that these are often forgotten in the impatience to do a deal.

If you meet this style in your negotiations, expect an enjoyable experience. You will need to be fully prepared, however, and ready to move quickly with new lines of thought and discussion. If you want repeatable deals, be sure to come through with whatever you have promised. You will be lucky to be given a second chance if you fail the first time. Great store is set by personal integrity and the keeping of promises.

The Germanic approach, which might include the negotiating styles of Holland, Denmark, Switzerland and Austria as well as Germany, is also seen generally to be strong and competent, but in a very different manner from the North American approach. The Germanic type of negotiator will generally be very controlled and inclined to be assertive, having planned formally and systematically in advance a view of exactly how things should be run. There will therefore be less flexibility in such negotiators' positions, and a greater reluctance to compromise. It should also be said that many foreigners find this style not only very tough, but on occasions also low on trust.

If the above describes you, you will probably be used to winning good deals, but will also find yourself more often than most in deadlock, with the end result sometimes being lose-lose. For example, I witnessed negotiations where a leader of a German sales team refused to concede a technical matter on principle, not because it was not a good point, but because it was

166

outside his 'official' sphere of competence. Without exception, opposing sales teams from France, Italy, Sweden and the UK all accepted the technical point willingly, because they saw it was of low cost to them but very high value to the other side, even though they also were not officially empowered to offer such a concession. Quite soon after this, the German sales team were told they were no longer in the running for the order.

This was partly because of the Germans' unwillingness to concede the technical point, but also because the other side felt that this was a bad portent. If the German sales team would refuse to agree such an important point *before* the business was placed, it was reasoned, then surely agreement on any other matter that might arise *after* the contract was signed would be even more dificult to resolve. If you find that you are in situations such as this, with the danger of lose-lose on the horizon, consider opening up broader ranges of options that will still meet your ends.

Aganst such a style, you need to be equally well prepared, and able to make maximum use of your exploration time. After that, if your point of view is ignored and seems to have little impact, you in turn may have to be prepared to use recess and deadlock.

One final tip from my own German colleagues: be punctual!

The French approach is seen as having great flair and intellectual fortitude. This means that matters tend to be treated very imaginatively, but also rigorously and firmly. Expect skilful use of emotion and a ready ability to say '*Non*', whether the apparent strength of that party justifies obstinacy or not. (I shall never forget a little cameo of a negotiation I witnessed at an amateur football match in the Ardennes. One linesman, who kept on raising his flag for 'off-side', was continually being over-ruled by the referee. Each time, there were long arguments between the two officials. In the end,the offended party could abide the rebuff no more. He threw down his flag and walked off. An excellent display in brinkmanship. What did the referee do? Not to be upstaged, he did the same thing: he also threw down his whistle and stormed off the pitch.)

The problem with this style of negotiation is that it can be very strong in win-lose situations, but not always very cooperative in win-win. If this style is close to your own, recognise that this will not always be to your advantage and listen more carefully to the other side's signals.

When you meet such a style, be prepared for either a sharp precise scalpel which will dissect a weak case easily, or an emotional whirlwind which you will want to let run its course before seeking progress. Some foreigners will also tell you that, despite all the above, even the most heated debate will be interrupted for the *casse-croute* (meal-break). (I don't accept this stereotype, myself, but then, when I worked in France, the common view of the English was that they were always taking a tea-break!) If your opposite numbers are indeed insistent upon breaking for a *grand répas*, then at least use the time as a helpful recess to diffuse some of the other side's energies – but not yours, if you can help it.

The Italian approach is seen as being strong in terms of using emotions, gestures and generally presenting a case, but not so good at listening to the other side. Many foreigners say they find that this makes win-win negotiations difficult, but in such cases there is another characteristic which can add to the problem: points already negotiated do not stay that way. Imaginative ways of circumventing agreements are also a feature of some parties (witness the increased output of some iron and steel products from Italy at a time when the European Commission had agreed that capacity would be cut). For those used to a southern Mediterranean culture, this is seen as being a perfectly reasonable negotiating stance.

If your style can be described this way, then the apparently unstructured approach you are labelled with *can* be very strong, but only when the other side is prepared to tolerate it. They may just walk away. The difficulty for you will be that the negotiating characteristics of other cultures will seem very unimaginative and plodding to you, but you will need to accustom yourself to this sometimes. The other side may in fact be offering you a very good deal, if you let them have some space in which they take the lead for a period of time.

If you encounter this style and you genuinely want to settle a deal, it is vital that you do not let the approach affect you emotionally. Either stay calm and stick to your guns, or prepare to match their style, but only if it comes naturally to you. Also, be prepared to take accurate notes, and summarise frequently.

The Hispanic approach may contain elements of the Italian or American methods described already. The reputation for procrastination (*'mañana'*) may be justified, but it is most usually used intentionally, when there is a tactical advantage to be gained. This style can be very pragmatic and is often strong in the exploration phase. Employing it can, however, lead negotiators into trapping themselves into making impossibly strong demands. Withdrawal is then either difficult, or generally weakens the rest of the case. When this happens, recess can be a very powerful tool, allowing for reconsideration and some way of saving face. The extended timescale often associated with such a negotiating style can often be a useful ally in these circumstances.

Many claim that this style is very good at negotiating key points, but that subsidiary matters tend to get forgotten. If you recognise this as a description of your own style, remember: keep the whole package in mind! If you face this style, many will tell you that for Spaniards in particular, there is much emphasis placed on personal contact, integrity and honour. They will also say that very often, the best intentions of formally confirming a deal get forgotten.

You may also be interested in the Spaniards' own view of regional stereotypes which, perhaps because of their history, are often strongly held prejudices. The Catalonians are seen by others as being very money-oriented (betraying Phoenecian origins?), the Basques are very strong on points of principle and ideals, while the Galicians are renowned for never answering questions directly. I have also been told that many Spaniards will, when asked, admit to a strong sense of 'pecking order' when dealing with foreigners. Nationalities from the economically or politically stronger parts of the world are viewed with a strong sense of inferiority; the rest with a defiant sense of superiority. If this is generally true, it clearly needs careful handling – once you have decided which category you belong to!

The Nordic approach might be characterised as being courteous, polite, quiet and helpful. (Even the Police are called the

'Politi' in Danish and Norwegian, but that may be due to no more than a linguistic accident!) In general, a climate which is open and helpful is preferred, where each side is encouraged to search for fresh angles on a problem and to propose innovative solutions. However, such a style is easily flattened by a more aggressive, brusque approach. This can then encourage a stubborn entrenchment of position, from which it will be difficult to move forward.

Naturally, there are many variations upon this theme. Many Swedes, it is said by others, adopt a more American approach. Some people find Swedish negotiators difficult to deal with. Indeed, many Swedes say that they generally see themselves as being well prepared and good at discussing detail. However, the difficulty that others report is probably more closely connected to a fact that many Swedes acknowledge: they like to be made to feel important, and in the spirit of true democracy, they all feel obliged to have their say. This may explain why they believe they make better buyers than salesmen!

Conversely, the Danish style is seen by other Scandinavians to be more appropriate for selling than buying, and indeed, Danes are often particularly tough negotiators. Danish colleagues tell me that, generally, they feel that the Danish negotiating approach more accurately falls within the Germanic category, already described.

Other Scandinavians usually say that they find the Finns the toughest, but also very fair, while they say Norwegians have a reputation for strong fellow-feelings, a certain narrowness of vision and (whisper it) laziness.

The advice to those who adopt a Nordic approach might be to continue to work hard at bringing out the other side's 'shopping list' at an early stage, but be prepared to be more assertive about presenting your own position when the time comes.

If you meet such an approach, recognise that a win-win outcome should not be difficult, but you may be tempted to fall into a competitive win-lose attempt which may well backfire on you unless it is very carefully prepared.

The Arabic approach is sometimes wrongly characterised by just one style. In fact the North African approach, for example, especially in Francophone Africa, is possibly more 'communist' in negotiating style (see below) than Arabic. Many Europeans claim that this particular style is very tough, cynical, ruthless and uncooperative (as opposed to many other parts of the 'dark continent', which are seen as being friendly, warm and generally cooperative). As another example, the style of the 'souk' will be more overt and aggressive than that in the office. It is important to recognise that these differences exist, or you may be in for some unpleasant surprises!

In Saudi Arabia, the Gulf areas and nearby, the overriding characteristic is the need for time, to allow for social niceties and a build-up of trust. The general business custom, rather than negotiating style in particular, is to allow frequent interruptions during discussions. This will require a high degree of patience from any Westerner. There is likely to be considerable personal pride involved in the negotiating position adopted, but the other side's skills will be fully respected. However, depending on locality, business attitudes are becoming increasingly Westernised with regard to negotiating style, and more akin to the American manner described above.

The Communist approach includes a variety of distinct but related styles. The national characteristics of East European countries are quite separately identifiable, as are those of other countries with Communist traditions, such as Cuba or the Republic of China. In general, however, the communist style is seen to reflect a pragmatic need to avoid, wherever possible, the taking of any personal responsibility for decision-making, especially if anything might possibly go wrong. The penalties for any mistakes can be very severe, by Western standards, which may account for a rather defensive view that 'they hunt in packs.' The Communist attitude therefore requires some sympathetic understanding, if you are going to be successful. It will also require patience, because of the attendant bureaucracy. It is also worth noting in passing, that in Eastern Europe, of all the major trading areas, female equality seems to be most strongly developed. Many negotiating teams will include, and may often be headed by, women.

To be successful, it is essential to allow time (which may be

171

thrust upon you, anyway; you may have to wait some time on arrival before being summoned for your appointment) for careful advance planning. You must be prepared to concede graciously 'interesting' amounts in several (pre-planned) slices, so that each member of the home side can claim some success. In many parts of the Communist world, their negotiators are purposely allowed almost no room for manoeuvre, so for them 'negotiation' is simply about drawing out concessions from you, rather than trading them. For this reason, it is especially important to build a sizeable negotiating margin into your initial offer.

A straw poll suggests that the Communist negotiating style is the toughest. Often, there will be political observers present to ensure 'correctness', so assume your interpreter (if provided officially, which will often be the case) might still be such an appointee, even if the influence of KGB-type secret police is now less prevalent.

Note that negotiation will continue right up to the final con-firmation stage. Indeed, in Cuba, a colleague was still badgered for additional discounts even *after* signing the deal, on his way back to the airport! He refused, politely of course. (In passing, it may be noted that the head of the Cuban delegation on this occasion was a woman.)

There is a very strong inclination in this style to say 'No' more often than usual, which makes for very difficult, if predictable, negotiations. A 'yes' from the other side is usually seen to be a sign that further concessions are available. The general character of this style is to prefer win-lose, as a 'natural' outcome of profes-sional negotiating, rather than win-win, which is often seen as being weak. To avoid this, it is important that you be prepared to invest in a long-term relationship with the intention of building on a platform of trust and goodwill, before developing business on any scale.

The very special atmosphere that is found in Eastern European countries appears to place a premium on strong one-to-one relationships. A friend made here is a friend for life, and a reward-ing personal relationship it will be. (Without in any way dimi-nishing this, however, you should also know that it is almost mandatory to 'look after' your Eastern Bloc contacts with small gifts of items that are not locally available, without of course making these with a view to corruption.) Because of the fear of making a mistake (which could include making a new arrangement that then failed), there is every incentive to continue with successful long-standing business relationships. This can make the long term investment, in time and patience, well worth while for those who are persistent.

The Far Eastern approach is seen variously as inscrutable, polite but ambitious, protracted and involved. Aspirations are invariably high, and always, great store is set by 'face' or self-respect. This is especially true amongst the Chinese. Apart from this aspect of face, negotiating in the Republic of China is not very dissimilar to dealing with other Communist countries, except that even more patience may be required.

Western methods of negotiation in some areas are still seen as suspect and untrustworthy, so a prolonged period of building up trust – possibly over many visits – is usually advisable. Those areas with greatest Western involvement (Japan, South Korea, Hong Kong, etc.) will be more used to 'Western' methods, but old traditions die hard. Courtesy and good manners are especially valued in this part of the world, and this includes being on time, dressing smartly and disagreeing only with the utmost respect and gentility. This sense of politeness extends to their being most reluctant to say 'No' to you, outright, and declining to say that they have not fully understood you, even when in fact they mean 'No', and haven't understood a word you have said. This can be most disconcerting, especially in countries such as Japan where a more Western approach might be expected to apply, given their great international exposure to world markets. Tremendous patience, resilience and resolve are essential in this part of the world, coupled with a sound understanding of 'face' and trust, and the empathy to ensure that neither side is put at risk by losing.

The Australian approach is robust, but open. There is a very polished variety, tough and 'no-nonsense' which may owe its origins to the characteristics of European and North American negotiating influences. It is a style which is also shared by experienced South African and New Zealand business people.

There is, however, another equally 'no-nonsense' approach, which is overtly more aggressive and rough. I particularly relish the story of a colleague from Britain visiting an Australian customer to resolve a complaint. The 'welcoming' greeting from the customer was so rude that no publisher would dare print it, but it included references to both his parentage and the likelihood or otherwise of continuing the family line. Fortunately, my colleague is no delicate flower himself and responded with a stream of jocular invective that would have turned the air a rich purple, if it wasn't already. From then on, my colleague and his customer became firm friends and concluded a deal that met all the requirements of both parties.

Judged by the outcomes that many report, this particular style has great merit, in that it is open and usually very 'fair' – a concept that is not a characteristic of all parts of the world!

The Indian approach (which extends over the whole sub-continent) is seen to be yet again quite different. Outsiders will remark most on the constant haggling, an approach that the skilled negotiator might applaud, for everything, however unlikely, is seen as negotiable. Claims are also often seen by others to be exorbitant, backed up by little of what Westerners see as 'logic'. Further, points once settled do not always stay that way, but equally, proposals for solution can grow in ingenuity and imagination as they are developed.

It is important to keep very accurate records of what has been agreed when you meet this style, and to build first on the desire (or otherwise) of the other party to conclude a deal. This will be helped by building up mutual respect and trust, with considerable funds of tolerance and understanding. Experience shows that it may often be prudent to let *them* do most of the talking in the bidding phase, while you maintain a frosty silence, at least initially. This can be a good tactic for reducing the more unreasonable demands you might encounter.

Summary

- In order to learn how best to cope with other personality types, it is important first to know yourself.

- Popular characterisations of others, their jobs and their negotiating styles, may be unhelpful stereotypes. Avoid these broad characterisations whenever you can.

- Nevertheless, it is important to make what assessments you can of the approach and style with which you expect to be confronted, and prepare accordingly.

Useful Exercise

- Practise matching your own assessments of personal and cultural styles with those of others, and pool this information on a team basis when planning.

10

SUMMARY, PITFALLS AND PRACTICE

'Experience is the mother of wisdom.' *Proverb.*

At the beginning of this book, we discussed the social inhibitions which many people feel about negotiating. With these inhibitions and misconceptions out of the way, we moved on to review the very wide range of skills which are appropriate for each stage of the bargaining process.

The difficulty we now have to face is how to remember such a large array of skills, so that they become almost second nature to us. We also need to ensure that we know how to use them with maximum impact.

Fortunately, the two problems have a common solution: practice. Only through experience can the practical importance and relevance of new skills become apparent. By practising these in role-playing exercises, where the outcome is not important, skills can be polished and put into context at the same time. Some suggestions for role-playing exercises follow.

First, however, let us review in summary form some of the more important points we have discussed so far, to ensure that the best deal possible is won. We should also highlight where problems might be encountered, and how they might be overcome. You will find the following a useful check list, whether your negotiations are practice role-plays or for real.

Preparing

- Don't be afraid to negotiate. But note that negotiating skills cannot give you power, if you have none to start with.

- The first offer is rarely the best. But to improve upon it, you have to ask.

- You have nothing to lose by asking for a better deal. Most things are negotiable.

- Propose solutions or remedies. Don't just complain.

- Check out your assumptions. Then test them.

- Prepare fully, and with care. Preparation and planning lie at the heart of a successful negotiation. Don't be caught out by having to do quick deals.

- Build a power-base, whether real or apparent, and use it. Be prepared to use brinkmanship as a vital tactic to win a power battle.

- Decide if your aim will be win-lose or win-win. Can you expect to win the best deal with a competitive style, where you look to maximise your slice of the bargaining cake, or will your best strategy be to aim for a cooperative sharing approach?

- Don't negotiate if you are not prepared.

- Don't negotiate if you don't have to, i.e. unless *you* have something to gain.

- The most successful side will usually be the one with the highest aspirations.

- Formalise your objectives, and your priorities. Know what you have to offer, its cost to you and its value to the other side. Be strong-minded and objective in setting your fall-back position (or 'limit'), beyond which you will not go in making concessions.

- Know what the other side will want, and what they might like.

- Establish the cost to you of what the other side may want, as well as its value to them.

- Estimate what the other side's opening bid is likely to be, compare it with where you believe settlement should be achieved, and thus calculate what your opening offer might be, by reference to the mid-point. If your opening offer, by implication, is likely to be damagingly unacceptable, consider the consequences of deadlock, or conceding in smaller steps than the other side.

- Find out who will be on their side, and decide who should be on your side. Ensure that your side reflects the integrity and credibility necessary to enforce your power-base.

- Allocate team duties to ensure the necessary blend of functional skills and personal skills. Nominate a leader, a note-taker and a reviewer.

- Make sure you have the support of your colleagues back at base. The last thing you want to do is to negotiate a deal that will then be undermined by your own side.

What can go wrong if you do all this? The most likely possibility is that you might still be taken by surprise. (Make sure that it is not a member of your own team who surprises you!) If you are surprised, be prepared to call a recess. Don't feel you have to 'play it by ear'.

One form of surprise might be that, even with the best inside knowledge available, the other side's requirements were not what you expected. In such cases, it is vital that you be flexible, in re-thinking your strategy to meet the new circumstances. That is, be agile in recognising that a different game plan may be necessary. It is rather pointless offering concessions that are of only minor interest to the other side while actually ignoring their key issues, for example.

One of the best ways to avoid surprises is to role-play your negotiation with friendly opposition. This takes time, but it will add immensely to your confidence as well as increasing your chances of being able to handle unexpected contingencies. For any important negotiation, this should form a standard part of your preparation.

You might fear that the other side is not willing to negotiate with you. If you have planned a well prepared power-base, then use it. How you do this will depend on whether you are ready for a win-lose negotiation (where you will use it blatantly, if you have to), or prefer to aim for a win-win solution (where any threats will need to be well-masked by adroit signalling).

Opening

- Be warm and positive in your opening. First impressions are important. Negative, hostile or aggressive opening statements will, in nearly every case, result in a similarly negative response. A basic requirement for a successful negotiation is mutual trust. Therefore be firm and fair.

- State who you are, what you hope to achieve, and how much time you have. Then agree an agenda. Setting a timescale should help accelerate reluctant concessions from the other side, later on. Once the agenda has been agreed, it is then quite reasonable for you to withdraw concessions should the other side later decide to bring in new issues.

- Signal your intentions clearly. Listen and watch carefully for their signals.

- Review seating arrangements. Try to avoid face-to-face confrontation. If you are not happy with the conditions arranged for you by someone else, seek to change them.

The opening phase of any negotiation usually sets the scene for what will follow. It is therefore worth giving it special attention and thought.

If problems arise at this stage, most commonly it is because of what has already happened. Misunderstandings that have occurred before the actual negotiation starts can sour the attitudes of even the most cooperative negotiators very easily. To avoid this, the opening phase may best be carried out before you meet. If the meeting was arranged on the telephone, you might sketch out an agenda and timescale then, making sure that you have elicited all the points which *they* want to cover, as well as those which you had in mind.

If the other side declines to accept your cordial approach, do not reply in kind. Continue to be polite and courteous. This will give you the moral high ground and enhance your underlying control of the situation.

A rather different problem can be deciding when to move from the opening phase on to the next one. This should not present a skilled negotiator with much difficulty, because it is to your advantage to open (and thus control) the next stage, which is exploration. You can do this quite easily by asking questions.

Initially, your questions can be quite 'innocent', as a prelude to making them more specific or pointed.

Exploring

- Test your assumptions. This should come naturally from setting the agenda.

- Identify the other side's decision-maker. If someone in authority is not present, then try and establish who the decision-maker is and ask if he or she can join you.

- Persuade them to set out their complete agenda, or 'shopping list' of wants. You don't need to make any specific comment at this stage. Your intention is to stop them adding new items later ('salami slicing'). Don't let detailed debate start at this stage, but make a note and say you will return to the point when their agenda of points has been fully drawn up. If you can, check out their priorities: what do they want most?

- Reveal as little as possible about the facts of your position. Concentrate instead on your feelings (whether true or stage-managed).

- Establish whether your win-lose or win-win preference, which you determined at the planning stage, was appropriate.

- Explore areas of common ground if you are seeking a win-win solution.

- Exploit your power-base.

If the other side manoeuvres you into having your position explored first, do not despair. Just make sure that you do not give too much away. If you are in a strong position, this is an excellent opportunity to aim high and develop your aspirations for the best deal going, which will lead naturally to the next stage (bidding). This might be a little premature, though, so be prepared, therefore, to make time to explore their position first, if there is any doubt about it in your mind. This will guard against any unpleasant surprises later on.

It is just possible that when you explore the other side's position, you may find that they haven't done their planning, or that there is internal dissent in their own camp.

If they have not properly prepared their case, it is up to you to lead. It is a fragile position to be in if you force a conclusion that will be revoked later. However, as long as you keep this thought in mind, in all other respects you are in a very strong position.

If there *is* internal dissension on the other side, you have to establish who holds the real power, then determine who is more prone to favour your viewpoint and try to promote harmony between those two parties. This situation calls for great diplomacy. If you weigh-in heavily on the side of one party, the other may see this as proof that their side is right in voicing opposition. However, with care, you should always be able to turn this division in their ranks to your advantage in the end, although a settlement may take much longer to achieve. If necessary, allow *them* time to recess.

Bidding

- Remember! Only proposals can be negotiated. Arguments can only (at best) support a case. If you are going to argue against the other side, do so coolly and logically, building up to a conclusion that can only result in one outcome: justified opposition on your part. Do not express disagreement first and *then* try to justify it.

- Keep a close watch on the mid-point, where appropriate.

- Concede slowly, in small amounts with limited authority, and show pain at your 'losses'.

- Make initial concessions small and tentative.

- Persuade the other side that your best-hoped-for outcome is actually the *least* you can possibly accept.

- Listen carefully.

- Talk in strong 'pictures', with confidence.

- Reward signals, not intransigence. When you receive a signal, explore it.

- Listen to the 'music behind the words'.

- Be prepared to deadlock.

- Don't block arguments. They need to be addressed. If in doubt, recess.

- Be ready to change the timing, the tempo, the topic, and even the team.

- Use deadlines to accelerate the offering of concessions.

- Don't let approaching deadlines lead you into making large concessions.

- Summarise regularly. Use the power of recess.

- Leave the other side thinking that *they* have won a good deal.

- Unrealistic proposals can be damaging.

- Interrupting proposals provokes argument. Instead, sit back, listen and take notes which you can refer to later.

- State firm and specific conditions first before making broad non-specific proposals.

- Aim high with your proposals. Make your highest aspirations sound like the *least* you can accept.

- Remember! The weakest party will usually make the first concessions.

- The first offer will rarely be the best available.

- Be prepared to say 'No', regularly.

- Search out as many variables as you can. You can then use these to extract further concessions.

- Trade concessions, seeking valuable ones, preferably in return for ones that cost you little (but may be of high value to the other side).

- Keep the whole deal in mind.

- Link issues into a package. Split a package into pieces.

- Make them justify their proposals.

- Flinch when you receive concessions.

- Don't gloat over a valued concession once you have extracted it. Keep a poker face.

- When you conclude, check what you have both agreed and ratify it. Assuming you wish a deal to be binding, ensure that it is legally enforceable.

These are long lists of points to remember and, of course, it would require a super-human effort to do so on the first reading. That is why practice is so important. At the end of each negotiation, you will find it helpful to re-read this section so you can check how well you performed. It will also serve as a useful reminder before you enter your next negotiation.

There is yet more you need to know, however, before we move on to the role-playing exercises. Over the centuries of human negotiations, a number of rather wily tricks have been invented, which you need to guard against, and above all, use for your benefit.

GAMES PEOPLE PLAY

Some of the gambits have already been referred to, but you will find it useful to have these summarised here, with others that have not been touched upon:

'Your place or mine?' Which is to *my* greater advantage? (Usually your place, as long as you can control telephone calls and other interruptions).

'Please sit here.' Only if it suits you.

'Limited authority.' Two can play at that game! Find out who does have authority.

'It isn't our policy.' This is a version of limited authority. It can be in the form of 'We've never done it that way before'. It is strong because it removes the personal responsibility from the negotiator and leaves the other side jousting at windmills. To overcome this, you *must* challenge. If you can't get the policy changed, you must ask for a special exception to be made, 'just this once'. (Any manager of a bureaucratic organisation with many genuine policy rules, will still tell you that exceptions are made – and hidden or excused – all the time, when necessity drives.)

'Salami slicing.' Avoid, by getting their complete shopping list of wants, and keeping the whole deal in mind.

'Say nothing.' You can do this too. Get used to silence and play it their way, if you have to.

'Time is running out.' This is a very powerful method of making intransigent negotiators move towards settlement. If someone does this to you, set a new deadline, for preference.

'Come back tomorrow.' This is a 'deadline in reverse', in the sense that the negotiation is wilfully prolonged. As with the 'Time is running out' ploy, it is designed to speed up or enhance settlement. It is especially useful with door-to-door salesmen, where you do want to buy, but at a better price. If you are on the receiving end of this, you may have no option but to comply or concede.

'I'm very angry.' Oh dear! Hear them out for a while. Don't interrupt and do be prepared to be very polite. Don't ignore their points, but be prepared to rebut them, calmly but firmly.

'The feint.' It turns out that they couldn't really care less about what you have just spent ages debating. No matter. Make sure you are equally firm on the real issues too.

'The snow job.' This is American slang for having the wool pulled over your eyes, usually to divert you from the very good point you have just made. It is the job of the 'note-taker' to make sure you return to it, before you both forget what your point was. It can also be used to divert you from taking up an issue at all, which might be damaging to the other side. Make sure you check regularly with your planning notes, to ensure that you have not inadvertently missed making all your best points. Summarising regularly will also help.

'Full disclosure.' It is usually nothing of the sort. It is on the same level as 'I'll be perfectly honest . . .', and you wouldn't fall for that, would you?

'Cobblers!' A meaningless denial which, it is hoped, will brook no argument. Probe further. 'What would you like us to understand by that remark?' can be a healthy prelude to asking them to justify it.

'Interruptions.' 'A phone call for you, Mr Smith'. 'Will you just sign this, Mr Smith?' 'There's another visitor, Mr Smith.' 'Would you like coffee now?' etc. Be patient and ignore them. Recognise that these interruptions are designed to put you off. Don't let them.

'Hawk and Dove.' This is also known as the 'White Hat, Black Hat' ploy. One party is very aggressive. Then the other turns very conciliatory and 'reasonable'. This is to encourage you to try and work harder for a solution with 'Mr Nice'. If you see things his way, he thinks he can persuade his mean, nasty colleague to keep quiet. How kind! Unfortunately for you, 'Mr Nice' wants your last penny just as much as 'Mr Nasty'. If you have built up your power base and have other proposals to make, ignore his entreaties. Ask, if he is so nice, why can't he accept your counter proposals?

'The Bluff.' Everyone will try this, even down to faking evidence, with false telexes or letters . . . Some people are predictably inclined to bluff, so you might safely assume that any suspect statement from them is almost certainly false. Some times you won't be sure. All you can do is to probe, challenge and seek proof. You may also have to give the bluffer a chance to save face, if you were right.

'Heads I win, tails you lose.' This is known as the 'alternative close' by salesmen. You are invited to choose between two options selected by the other side, neither of which may be to your liking, e.g., 'The new machine you sold us only runs at half speed. Will you cut your bill by half, or would you rather take the goods back?' *Your* job is to search for other variables. That way, you don't have to choose theirs. You might reply to the above: 'We'll do neither. We'll send an engineer round to put it right for you.'

'The Emotional Appeal.' Someone makes you a powerful request to do something, that is founded on emotion rather than logic (or even the contract). If you are a 'sucker', you will fall for the bait and accept. If you are an 'evil, heartless brute', you won't. You can't win this one, whichever course you take! The best response is to make an equally emotional claim.

'Cassandra.' The 'If you don't do as I ask, the end of the world will happen' style of negotiating is crude and juvenile, but for all that, it works rather well if it is matched by a strong power-base! If your position is genuinely weak, there isn't much to negotiate about. More often, however, this will be an attempt at crude coercion rather than a statement of fact. Ask 'Are you threatening me?' Few will say 'Yes', but if they do, you have the moral upper hand which will justify a request that they withdraw the threat. Alternatively, *you* can threaten to complain to a higher authority or to walk out.

'OTT (Over the Top).' This is 'Aim High!' to the point of total annihilation. Their demand is completely unreasonable, but you don't want to walk out (the best response). There are three options. One is a logical debate as to why it is unreasonable. Another is to reply with an equally unrealistic counter-offer. This is not very 'adult'. The third option is therefore a variation on the second. Accept their offer, but *link* it with an equally unreasonable condition.

'Independent Observers.' How did you guess? They aren't *really* independent. Be suspicious of uninvited guests and ask them to identify themselves fully at the beginning.

'By the way . . .' This is a tactic much loved by some interviewers, as well as negotiators. 'By the way', they say as they walk with you to the exit, your mind now concentrating on where you left the car, or how you are going to get back home. They then hit you with a question they know most would not answer honestly ('What do you think of us, then?') or, in the case of a negotiation, a last minute demand ('By the way, you will be holding your prices through to next year, won't you?'). The idea is to catch you off-guard. It works every time, too, until you learn to expect it.

USEFUL PHRASES – AND OTHERWISE

We have already said that clear communication, in strong but simple language, is an important part of good negotiating. Here are some useful phrases you can try on appropriate occasions:

'I'm sure we can settle this.'
'May I suggest that we agree an agenda first?'
'How long do we have together today?'
'I would propose . . .'
'What other points will you want to raise . . .?'
'Before we discuss that in detail, can you tell us . . .?'
'What if . . .?' 'Suppose we . . .?' 'Why don't you . . .?'
'If you were to . . ., then we might consider . . .'
'As things stand, we couldn't . . .'
'Could you tell us quite what you mean by . . .'
'So what you are saying is . . .'
'What special problems would you have if . . .?'
'My boss wouldn't let me . . .'
'You wouldn't seriously expect us to . . .'
'That would seem to us to be a rather hostile proposal. Could you please explain why you think it is reasonable to ask us to . . .?'
'If we could settle this point, would we be in a position to do a deal?'
'Would it be helpful if we summarised what has been said so far?'
'What would you say were the key issues which divide us?'

There are also some phrases you will want to avoid, e.g., 'Impossible', 'No way', 'With respect', 'You must be mad', and similarly unhelpful comments. Also to be avoided are a number of phrases that you will hear people say in the heat of the moment. They are clearly very unprofessional, in the context of a negotiation, because of what they give away. Here are some of the worst examples:

'Have you got any . . .? We must have some urgently.'
'We can't get it anywhere else.'
'Our works engineer thinks your product is the best on the market.'
'Your offer was very reasonable.'
'Our purchasing people will send you an order.'

'Send me your cancellation charges.'
'Let me know if our price isn't competitive.'
'When would you like to pay for this?'

PRACTICE

The best role-playing exercises are the ones closest to the circumstances in which you are about to negotiate. You can then include all the side issues, personalities and so on that you might expect to meet. Especially important, you can more easily put yourself into the other side's position. This *role reversal* is a very important tool in gauging the other side's point of view before a serious negotiation. When making your initial asessment of their position and requirements, it is very easy to become too bound up with your *own* side's perception of the key issues. When seen from *their* point of view, things may begin to look very different. It is clearly better to take this into account at the planning stage, rather than in mid-negotiation.

For general practice and training, it is important in the early stages to keep the number of issues for debate to a minimum in order to avoid confusion. There is another less obvious advantage to this, too. If several people engage in the same exercise successively, they will be astounded at the variety of outcome that is possible, depending upon individual styles and approach. The simpler the case, the more powerfully this point is demonstrated. A good example for demonstrating this is the following role-play:

The Trader. One team is asked to sell an article, almost anything you care to nominate, to another team, who in turn will have to sell it on in due course. The aim of each side is to secure for themselves the greater trading profit.

The buying team is told how much they can expect to *re-sell* the article for, and instructed therefore to buy at the lowest possible price, so that their re-sale margin is as large as possible. Naturally, they do not know what the sales team had to pay for the article in the first place.

The selling team is told, separately, the original *cost price* and

189

Role reversal is an important tool in gauging the other side's point of view.

instructed to sell the article to the buying team for the best price they can get. While they do not know what their purchaser's re-sale price might be, they clearly have to recognise that the other side will also have to make an acceptable profit, when they sell the article in their turn.

Classic laboratory-based trials have usually used a secondhand car as the article to be negotiated for in this type of exercise, with an initial cost price to the selling team of $2,500, and a re-sale price onward from the buying team of $3,500. The mid-point, where well-matched players would expect to settle, is $3,000. A range from $2,501 to $3,499 is of course possible.

It is particularly instructive to plot each side's initial offer, the number of moves they make, and the size of each move. Especially imaginative players will seek to enhance their power by introducing new variables, such as special payment terms, a guarantee, a 'free' service, assistance with advertising the subsequent sale, a trade-in, 'information' (imagined) about the state of the market, possibly a re-spray and so on. Although the case study is expressed in simple terms, there is nothing wrong with the role-players seeking to add new dimensions. After all, this is exactly what happens in real life.

After some practice with 'The Trader', a slightly more complex game in terms of stated variables can be used. As an example, let's take the 'Insurance Claim', which was referred to in Chapter 1. The debating points are how much was lost in a burglary, and how much should be covered by insurance. Most other complications are left to the imagination of the role-players. Each side is briefed separately, along these lines:

Insurance Claim. The two competing parties are lawyers seeking an out-of-court settlement. The claimant has been burgled and has lost a number of valuables, including a set of matching diamond rings and ear-studs. The exact value of all the items lost is in doubt, partly because there was not an exact register of all the valuables. This was primarily the claimant's fault, although the insurance company had been advised some time ago that there was doubt about the total value. This letter was merely acknowledged by the insurance company, without further detailed advice. Unfortunately, the burlary had occurred before the items could all be valued professionally. However, the value of the diamond jewellery alone is acknowledged to be worth at least $100,000. Other items may in total be worth many times this and at least another $100,000.

Apart from the uncertainty over the value of the net loss, there is also doubt over whether the claimant had adequately protected his property on the evening of the burglary. The claimant was known to be a little absent-minded and there was no sign of a forced entry. The insurance company's lawyers are aware of this, and will take it into account, but they have also been told privately that the claimant is an exceptionally good customer, whom they do not wish to lose. The client was insured in total for losses of several millions, so the actual loss was only partial.

Both parties are told to negotiate the best deal for their side, and that deadlock is not permitted because the costs of going to court will be unacceptable to either party.

This is a 'fun' exercise, designed to highlight the importance of some of the key skills. Participants are encouraged not to be too concerned about whether the detail of the situation described is very realistic or not. In practice, however, those involved do become very caught up in their own side's imaginary case. Some continue arguing even after the 'game' is over.

The lawyers for the claimant will seek to maximise their client's loss. They will no doubt wish to stress that the client had advised the insurance company that the value of the goods was uncertain, but that the company had not then chosen to withdraw cover. A very high sum should be sought. Many will start at $1 million or more.

The lawyers for the insurance company will of course deny any claims for goods of uncertain value, or unproven existence. They will also wish to suggest negligence by the other side's client, and propose the smallest settlement they think they can get away with. Many will offer less than $100,000.

At this stage, both parties will need to explore each other's case and search for variables. The claimant will want to stress that if the offer is so low, he has been paying far too high a premium. The insurance company will then talk about its conditions relating to partial loss and the onus upon the owner to prove the value of items lost. The claimant will no doubt start to talk of taking his insurance business elsewhere, writing to the press, etc. In response, the insurance company will probably want to explore further the ease with which the goods had been stolen, possibly the condition of the goods allegedly lost, and so on.

When it comes to settling, imaginative negotiators usually want to bring a number of invented variables into the bargaining (the claimant may have unexpectedly found photographs or old receipts for the valuables that have been stolen; the insurance company may have found from old files that the owner has a record of claiming for stolen goods that have only been mislaid. Perhaps they can advise the other side that their client has a criminal record (where did the money come from in the first place?) and threaten to call in the police, etc.

The outcome is generally somewhere between $150,000 and $250,000, often on the strength of a threat to withdraw future business. However, very high aspirants win settlements as low as $75,000 for the insurance company ('and we consider that to be a very generous gesture, Sir. May we suggest you have new locks fitted and a burglar alarm installed?), and as high as $750,000 for the claimant.

Occasionally, the parties will lose sight of the necessity of doing a deal and deadlock. (This is not surprising. On one occasion, the 'insurance company' refused to move above $15,000, and the 'claimant' would not consider accepting less than $1,000,000!)

Longer and more complex role-playing exercises can be developed to order. However, if too many issues are brought in, the benefit of the role-play tends to be lost as each side struggles to understand all the detail, rather than build up a sound strategy.

In commercial negotiations, untutored participants often ignore all issues other than price. In order to demonstrate the spread of other variables available for trading, specific case studies can be constructed. Let's look briefly at just two examples:

House Purchases. These make instructive case studies, especially if the financial requirements of each party are strictly defined. This then forces each side to concentrate on seeking non-financial variables with which to trade. These can include negotiations over carpets, curtains, furniture, moving-in dates, the funding of bridging loans, help with the mortgage or insurance, advice on local schools and amenities, introductions to the local golf club, use of a holiday villa overseas, retention or other-wise of prize plants in the garden, redecoration, re-direction of mail, introductions to neighbours, dentists, doctors, milkmen, etc. This is also a good exercise to practice either linking of issues and offering a package, or splitting the package up.

Large Contracts. These can make very involved, but useful, case-studies. The excitement comes in developing varying power bases at different stages, first for one side, then for another, by adding new elements as the negotiations unfold, such as last minute competition, a change in specification, a strike, price escalation, delivery delays, a failure by the customer to supply adequate facilities to permit installation, performance problems, etc.

Role-playing real-life situations is especially valuable when each party can identify closely with the issues and the personalities. The difficulty with practising these large case-studies comes in keeping track of everything that has happened and what people said (or didn't say). Closed-circuit television for such exercises, with video-recording, is an excellent way to solve this problem and also provides very helpful feed-back. It is amazing how many points are revealed on play-back, such as signals given but ignored, actions promised but not taken (e.g., one side proposes a recess, but is then diverted into a new argument), things said but not believed (wrong body language), offers made but not accepted, and so on. Even the most experienced negotiators can find such exercises helpful.

Appendix

CHECKSHEETS

Attached are some ideas to help you plan, record and monitor your negotiations. Experience shows that a formalised approach to this is useful in the early stages. However, many negotiators soon prefer to move away from the discipline that this planning routine demands. They then 'play it by ear' as a matter of course. You will no doubt make your own mind up about this, but it is interesting to note that many experienced negotiators do continue to use some kind of system, and they are probably more successful accordingly.

The preparation sheet is designed to encourage making some difficult judgements *before* the negotiation, rather than leaving them to chance. Not only does this mean matching the selection of your team to that which you expect the other side to field, it also demands an analysis of how you see your relative strengths and weaknesses, the balance of power and, accordingly, the probable objectives of each side. The variables in each side's position need to be identified, along with the associated costs and values to either side. These should give a clear idea of what each might – or might not – wish to concede. The opening stance and subsequent developments can then be planned, watching of course for pitfalls and traps on the way.

The record sheet is designed to ensure that assumptions are checked out, that the other side's full 'shopping list' is obtained and prioritised, and that each move in the subsequent sequence of trading is recorded and monitored. In complicated negotiations, it is naturally difficult to encapsulate all the deals into one mid-point, but keeping an eye on the balance of the trading is an excellent discipline. If you need time to do some calculations during the course of your discussions, don't be reluctant to ask for a recess. This may well save problems later on. The final outcome needs to be confirmed, by both parties, together with a list of agreed actions, as appropriate.

The analysis sheet is designed to review whether the initial objectives are met, whether assumptions were checked and where the eventual balance of power lay. The emphasis should be on learning for the next time. The form is worth filling in with ruthless honesty. Experience shows that very few negotiators will naturally believe they could have done better, without this.

In completing these checksheets, you might care to remember the moral of this book:

A better deal is nearly *always* possible!

NEGOTIATION PREPARATION SHEET

1	MEETING WITH .... AT .... ON						
2	**PRINCIPALS:** US			THEM			
	Name	Title	Role	Name	Title	Style	Authority
a	....			....			
b	....			....			
c	....			....			
d	....			....			

3 MAIN TOPICS:

A ....

B ....

C ....

4 SUBSIDIARY ITEMS:

D ....

E ....

F ....

5	**STRENGTHS:** (Exploit) Our	**WEAKNESSES:** (Exploit) Their

---

6	**WEAKNESSES:** (Shield) Our	**STRENGTHS** (Real?) Their

---

7 BALANCE OF POWER:

8	**HOW IS OUR POWER BASE**	**HOW IS THEIR POWER BASE**
A	To be developed?	A To be reduced?
B	To be exploited?	B To be verified?

9	**OUR OBJECTIVES:**		
A	MUST HAVE	Value to us	Cost to them
1	....	....	....
2	....	....	....
3	....	....	....
B	WOULD LIKE		
4	....	....	....
5	....	....	....
6	....	....	....
C	OTHER CONCESSIONS (we might like)		

10	**THEIR OBJECTIVES**	Cost to us	Value to them
A	MUST HAVE		
1	....	....	....
2	....	....	....
3	....	....	....
B	WOULD LIKE		
4	....	....	....
5	....	....	....
6	....	....	....
C	OTHER CONCESSIONS (we might offer)		

11   WIN-WIN OR WIN-LOSE?

12	**STANCE/TACTICS**	Us	Them
A	OPENING BID		
B	DEVELOPMENTS		

NEGOTIATION RECORD SHEET

1   MEETING WITH .... **AT** .... **ON** ....

PRINCIPALS	US		THEM		
Name	Title	Role	Name	Title	Role
a	....		a	....	
b	....		b	....	
c	....		c	....	
d	....		d	....	

2   ASSUMPTIONS   True/False

....

....

....

....

3	**OUR SHOPPING LIST**	Priority	**THEIR SHOPPING LIST**	Priority
a	....		a	
b	....		b	
c	....		c	
d	....		d	
e	....		e	
f	....		f	
g	....		g	

4	**SEQUENCE**	US	Mid-Point	THEM
i				
ii				
iii				
iv				
v				
vi				
vii				
viii				
ix				
x				
xi				
xii				

5   OUTCOME   Confirmed?

6 ACTION NEEDED	By Whom	By When

NEGOTIATION ANALYSIS

1 WERE OBJECTIVES ACHIEVED?	WON		LOST	
	Value to us	Cost to them	Cost to us	Value to them
a				
b				
c				
d				
e				
f				
g				
h				

2 NET BALANCE:

3 WERE OUR ASSUMPTIONS CHECKED?	Right	Wrong	Not checked
a			
b			
c			
d			
e			

4 POWER   US   THEM

5 STYLE:

6 HOW COULD WE HAVE DONE BETTER? (Note: most people will feel they did well – win or lose)

7 PERSONAL PERFORMANCE: US (to learn from)	THEIRS (for when we next meet)
a	
b	
c	
d	

8 FUTURE ACTION:

Signature(s):   Date:

SUGGESTED READING

There are many books on negotiating; they are (nearly) all worth reading, even if only to test your own skills against the authors'. It is an arrogant person who would claim to know it all! For an excellent review of some of the academic research on negotiating, and a lead into this particularly fascinating world, I can recommend for its accessiblity to the lay-person: *Negotiating Behaviour*, by Dean G. Pruitt, Academic Press.

On the subject of contract law, the authoritative text in the UK that is less than several inches thick (in fact, exactly 1 inch in paperback) is: *The Sale of Goods*, by Prof. P. S. Atiyah, Pitman Publishing.

As a commentary on the details of a commercial contract (without touching on the *practice* of negotiating *per se*, which makes it rather misleadingly titled), you may also find the following useful: *Successful Negotiation of Commercial Contracts: A Businessman's Guide*, by Patrick Hearn, Oyez Publishing.

You will have realised that understanding yourself and other people is an important feature of successful negotiating. Reference has already been made to: *I'm OK – You're OK*, by Dr. Thomas A. Harris, Jonathan Cape.

Reference was also made in Chapter 9 to various personality tests. A book worth reading by any manager, which includes further information on the subject of the 16 PF tests specifically, is: *Creating the Hands-On Manager*, by Bill Watts with Alison Corke, Mercury Books.

I can also recommend to anyone, on the related topic of assertiveness, even though it is obviously written for women: *A*

Woman in Your Own Right. Assertiveness and You, by Anne Dickson, Quartet Books; *Asserting Yourself*, by Dr. Marsha Linehan and Dr. Kelly Egan, Century Publishing; and *Conversation Control Skills for Managers*, by Prof. Charles Margerison, Mercury Books.

As an excellent introduction to the study of body language, both at work and play, you will enjoy: *Body Language*, by Allan Pease, Sheldon Press.

INDEX

Developing Your Career in Management

Jeremy G. Thorn

(PB, £9.99, 192pp, 216mm x 135mm, ISBN: 1-85252-176-7)

Developing a career in management does not just happen - it takes careful planning.

This book answers many of the questions which anyone seeking to develop a career in management needs to ask:

- What employers want from their managers.
- How a mentor can help.
- How to set career goals and retain flexibility.
- How to establish the right work relationship with your boss.
- What skills are required to manage others.
- How to handle office politics.
- Why networking is so important - and how to do it.
- How to turn problems into opportunities.

The author gives practical tips on how to stay in control of your career, how to turn disaster into opportunity, and how to seek excellence for yourself and your team.

ABOUT THE AUTHOR

Jeremy Thorn is managing director of Quantum Enterprise Development, a consulting firm specialising in management development and training. He is the author of several internationally published business books, including *The First-Time Manager* and *How to Negotiate Better Deals*, also available from Management Books 2000.

'This is a book that cannot be too strongly recommended for those with clear objectives in their management career - be they to get to the top, or merely to survive' *Professional Manager*

Available from leading booksellers.
To order by phone, ring 0235-815544 (credit cards accepted)

The First-Time Sales Manager

Jeremy G. Thorn

(PB, £7.50, 240pp, 216mm x 135mm, ISBN: 1-85252-050-7)

A complete introduction to sales management, targeted primarily at the newly appointed manager but also of relevance for anyone responsible for managing sales.

The book is packed with practical tips, advice and examples and fully supported with checksheets, working documents and useful exercises.

Subjects covered include:

- Managing - not selling: the difference between sales and sales management
- What a sales manager does: including recruitment, leadership, motivation, appraisal, strategy, reports, and forecasting
- Marketing and strategic direction: an introduction to basic marketing principles
- How to handle problems: examples and solutions

ABOUT THE AUTHOR

Jeremy Thorn, author of *How to Negotiate Better Deals* and *Developing Your Career in Management*, has managed sales forces as large as 300 and as small as one, selling products all over the world, to both industrial and consumer markets.

"A concise, easily readable guide which should become an indispensible aid both for the first-time sales manager himself, as well as for those employing him...An excellent publication that any company employing sales managers should use" *Business Review*

Available from leading booksellers.
To order by phone, ring 0235-815544 (credit cards accepted)

Lifeskills'
Personal Development Series

Lifeskills Communications

(All titles: PB, £4.99, 60-72pp,234mm x 153mm)

A series of mini-workbooks, aimed at helping readers to improve basic career and life management skills. Packed with self-tests, checklists and questionnaires.

Lifeskills Communications is one of Britain's leading training and consulting groups. Its teams of writers specialise in providing published materials on personal and skills development topics.

ASSERTIVENESS
'Demystifies and makes accessible techniques and approaches which could be of significant value to many people' *Training Officer*

COMMUNICATION
Designed to improve communication skills in and out of the workplace.

RELATIONSHIPS
A practical guide to the complex area of relationship management.

STRESS, HEALTH AND YOUR LIFESTYLE
Shows readers how to create a realistic and effective plan for stress management which could transform their lives.

TIME MANAGEMENT
A workbook for the development of crucial prioritising and time management skills.

TRANSITIONS
An essential guide to planning, managing and dealing with change.

Available from leading booksellers.
To order by phone, ring 0235-815544 (credit cards accepted)

Persuasive Business Presentations

Nick Robinson

(PB, £7.50, 128pp, 216mm x 135mm, ISBN: 1-85252-061-2)

This practical handbook contains a wealth of tested ideas to make your business presentation more powerful - and more profitable.

The book covers all aspects of successful presentation, including:

- preparing the script
- use and interpretation of body language
- stage management
- use of audio-visuals
- coping with disaster

Based on 25 years' experience of selling effectively though personal presentations.

ABOUT THE AUTHOR

As chairman of the Marketing Guild, and founding director of the marketing consultancy Datanews, Nick Robinson has led more than 300 conferences throughout Europe and the US, addressing groups from 100 to as many as 1000. He is also the author of *The Marketing Toolkit*, a practical guide to alternative marketing techniques (available from Management Books 2000 at £6.99).

"A valuable book for even the best of speakers. Lucid and lively." *Norman Hart, Chairman, International Foundation for Public Relations*

Available from leading booksellers.
To order by phone, ring 0235-815544 (credit cards accepted)